INTERPERSONAL SKILLS TRAINING

A HANDBOOK FOR FUNERAL SERVICE STAFFS

Alan D. Wolfelt, Ph.D.
Director
Center For Loss
and
Life Transition
Fort Collins, Colorado

ACCELERATED DEVELOPMENT
A member of the Taylor & Francis Group

INTERPERSONAL SKILLS TRAINING

A Handbook for Funeral Service Staffs

10 9 8
Reprinted September, 1992 with modifications.

Printed in the United States of America

Technical Development: Tanya Dalton
        Sue Davis
        Marguerite Mader
        Sheila Sheward

Library of Congress Cataloging-in-Publication Data

Wolfelt, Alan.
  Interpersonal skills training : a handbook for funeral service staffs / Alan D. Wolfelt.
    p. cm.
  Includes bibliographical references and index.
  ISBN 1-55959-025-4
  1. Undertakers and undertaking--Handbooks, manuals, etc.
 2. Interpersonal communication--Handbooks, manuals, etc.
 3. Interpersonal relations--Handbooks, manuals, etc. I.Title.
RA622.W65 1990
363.7'5--dc 20   90-84099
                  CIP

LCN: 90-84099

ACCELERATED/DEVELOPMENT
A member of the Taylor & Francis Group
7625 Empire Drive
Florence, KY 41042
1-800-634-7064

DEDICATION

To my many funeral director friends throughout the United States and Canada. It has only been through your encouragement, validation, and support that these materials have been refined to the point of maximum effectiveness for the learner. Thanks for participating in my workshops and challenging me to continue to share my thoughts and feelings about funeral service.

I like to think that funeral directors have, in part, helped me discover meaning in my life. Someone once said, "All of us are born for a reason, but all of us don't discover why. Success in life has nothing to do with what you gain in life or accomplish for yourself. It's what you do for others." I'd also like to think that this book will help funeral home staffs "do for others" to the best of their ability during one of life's most difficult of times.

A.D.W.

ACKNOWLEDGEMENTS

I wish to thank all of the people who encouraged me to write this book. Many of my funeral director friends throughout the United States and Canada have been supportive of my efforts to make a contribution to funeral service. Without them, this text would not have become a reality. Particular thanks go to Ken Parson and Garl Matchett who stimulated my initial interest in working with funeral directors.

Special thanks also go to participants in my workshops who have helped me explore and expand my thinking. They have helped me refine these materials to the point of maximum effectiveness for the learner.

The greatest debts of gratitude are owed to my wife, Susan, and daughter, Megan, for their understanding, patience, tolerance, encouragement, and love. These two bring meaning and purpose to both my personal and professional life.

August 1990   Alan D. Wolfelt, Ph.D.
                   Director of Training
                   Center for Loss and Life Transition
                   Fort Collins, Colorado

FOREWORD

At a national convention of Compassionate Friends, someone said words that I'll never forget: "Sometimes when just one person is missing the whole world seems so empty."

This is precisely when you, the funeral director, are called. Death has struck the family like a tidal wave. They are cut loose from their moorings and are all but drowning in the sea of their turbulent sorrow. As the bereaved are empty, so is the world around them.

At precisely this moment, many funeral directors are searching for their role-identity. "I'm a funeral director, not a counselor"—familiar words that both Dr. Alan Wolfelt and I have heard on too many occasions. We want to scream, "Look at the bereaved sitting before you. Part of them is being buried with their loved one. Pain and fear are washing over them in waves and they are wondering if they will ever survive. They are looking to **you** for consolation and guidance. The word **counselor** comes from the Latin **consilium** meaning "to consult." The survivors are there for your advice, suggestions, and experience. It's not a question whether you, the funeral director, like the word **counselor.** By definition, you are! The needy, empty people around you are there for **consultation.** The real question is whether you will be an effective counselor or not." "But I make a living out of funeral service, how then can I be a counselor?" is the next question we hear. So do helping professions like clergy, psychologists, psychiatrists, and social workers "make a living" by helping others. The word **profit** is not an evil word as the Soviet Union is now learning. A caring and knowledgable businessperson *can* be a warm and compassionate counselor.

Notice the word *can.* That is why Alan Wolfelt's book is destined to become a classic in its field. The truth is that many schools of mortuary science prepare the student on how to pass the state boards in anatomy and physiology. Too long have counseling and psychological techniques been conspicuous by the absence. As Mark Twain said: "It's not what people know that gets them in trouble but it's what they know that isn't so."

Dr. Wolfelt's informative and comprehensive book will teach you both practical and effective interpersonal skills that are so essential to your response to those who come to you when their world is empty. You will learn, together with your staff, how to listen more dynamically to both their verbal and non-verbal clues. As you test yourself by role-playing, sentence completion, and self-evaluation, you will learn much about yourself—your own genuineness, warmth, respect, empathy, and trust.

Dr. Wolfelt has devoted much of his creative career to children by reminding us that a person is a person no matter how small. One of the worst problems is youngsters' lack of understanding because of adult secrecy. They, too, need to express their emotions through the ceremonies of death—the wake, the funeral, the "shivah," the interment. Funeral directors are tenderly instructed on how to be sensitive to the age and level of each child.

Most important, Alan Wolfelt has written: "If you want to be more helpful to others, help yourself." Ralph Waldo Emerson said it differently: "Nothing can bring you peace but yourself." The book faces squarely the stresses of the funeral director and the impending signals of burnout. Some of the latest empirical studies now demonstrate that people with emotional overload are not those who necessarily work your long hours. Rather those who burn out are because of low self-esteem and sense of professional inadequacy. Both Dr. Wolfelt and I believe in the great work you are doing in ministering to those in agony and distress. We know that the research studies at the Harvard Community School of Psychiatry and the Clarke Institute of Psychiatry in Toronto rate you—the funeral director—as the *highest* among professionals in helping the bereaved. Now, you must believe it, too! With greater training in interpersonal skills, you will feel even better about yourself.

One final word: The final activity is "Moving Toward Closure: *Gift*-Giving." As I read this book, I began to understand that this marvelous book is not only for funeral directors, but for *all* people in their relationship to self, family, and community. We will *all* gain insights that will change not only our professional but our personal lives as well. I have grown as a result of this powerful volume. Dr. Alan Wolfelt, clinical thanatologist and educator, has given us a *gift* that can change our lives. As Chamfort said: "God comforts us that we may be better comforters."

> Rabbi Earl A. Grollman, D.D.
> Lecturer
> Author of "Living When a Loved One Has Died"

TABLE OF CONTENTS

LIST OF ACTIVITIES

LIST OF FIGURES

PART I

RECOGNIZING
THE ROLE
OF
INTERPERSONAL
SKILLS

CHAPTER 1

WHY THIS BOOK?

The impetus for this book came from the enthusiastic response of funeral home staffs who have discovered the rewards of learning effective interpersonal skills. Effective interpersonal or "helping skills" serve as the foundation upon which other life skills are developed. Sound funeral service practice is dependent on high levels of interpersonal communication.

This book is the culmination of the author's efforts to contribute to funeral service in a productive and, hopefully, meaningful way. My desire is that the contents be of value to both the student just starting out in funeral service and the experienced practitioner. For the student, this book is intended to provide a solid foundation in interpersonal skills training and their mastery. For the experienced funeral director, the book will serve as a resource for assessing current skills, adding new skills, and enhancing professional competence.

As a trainer of funeral home staffs I work from the conviction that all interpersonal relationships are either helpful (growth-enhancing), neutral (neither helpful or harmful), or harmful (destructive). I also believe that skills in responding helpfully to others are not innate, but learned through modeling and focused practice.

This book provides principles, practical skills, and activities whose aim is to enhance funeral home staffs' ability to respond helpfully to others. So, in essence, the contents of this text are directed at persons in funeral service who want to be more effective in working with people. My hope is that by the time you have completed this training program you will have some additional tools which will allow you to feel even more comfortable in your interpersonal relationships.

During my years as a college student and prior to becoming a person who works as a clinical thanatologist and educator, I had the distinct privilege of living and working in a progressive funeral home for seven years. As my own learning progressed, I began to teach funeral home staffs—both employers and employees—human relations or helping skills. What I discovered was a group of very caring people who had a true desire to find specific ways to better help people before, during, and after the funeral. I also discovered that when funeral home staffs worked together in an effort to learn interpersonal skills, their effectiveness and sense of satisfaction with their chosen profession of funeral service increased tremendously.

As I have traveled throughout the United States and Canada, training funeral directors, I'm always disappointed when I encounter that segment of funeral directors who firmly believe that "funeral directors are not and should not be counselors."

My own belief is that any funeral director who does not believe he or she "counsels" families might want to consider if this profession is really meant for him or her. This debate about "Is the funeral director a counselor?" goes beyond definitional semantics to the essential role of the funeral director.

Perhaps Howard Raether and Robert Slater (1975) responded to this question best when they wrote in their text, *The Funeral Director and His Role As Counselor*, that, "Most persons who notify the funeral director of a death and ask him to be of service are in essence saying, 'I have a problem; what should I do?' As soon as the funeral director acknowledges this notification and begins to give direction to the person or persons involved, he assumes the role of counselor."

There is no doubt that this long-lasting argument about the "funeral director as counselor" is based on how one defines counseling. If we define counseling in the following way, perhaps we can all agree that funeral directors are, in fact, counselors:

Counseling in funeral service is an interpersonal helping process designed to help one party or entire family gain insight into a problem and discover ways to cope with the problem.

A death within the family often creates crisis for the survivors. The survivors have a problem—confronting the death of someone loved. No other helping professional has the same level of intimate contact with the family at a time of death than the funeral director. Through his or her training and experience the funeral director offers counsel related to choices that help survivors cope with the death of someone loved. My experience suggests that compassionate and competent counsel can dramatically impact the long-term healing process of surviving family members. So, in summary, I believe the funeral director is a counselor. The question is whether he or she will be helpful, neutral, or harmful in the interpersonal arena.

A FOCUS ON SERVICE

Experience tells us that statements of appreciation following a funeral relate to personal service, not to equipment and caskets. This is an obvious reminder that the most important thing that you, the funeral director, have to offer is yourself.

The physician offers service. The minister offers service. The attorney offers service. And the most important thing that the funeral director has to offer is himself or herself.

The chapel, the couch, the limousine, and the music are worth little to the family without the person who by the experience, education, and concern helps make the funeral meaningful.

At a recent state convention I overheard a funeral director make the following comment: "I think I received the best funeral service education available, but it was education in the physical sciences and not training in helping the living people. In other words, at the same time I was being told the funeral was for the living, I was only being trained to care for the dead."

I have attempted to bring to this book what I believe is the most essential of interpersonal skills for funeral service personnel. You will not find in-depth theoretical discussion of the nature of helping relationships. You will not find technical jargon or lengthy quotations. What you will find, however, are practical and effective ways to feel more complete in your work as a funeral director.

So this book is an introduction to applied human relations whereby you will be encouraged to integrate your current knowledge with new skills in order to reach a higher level of interpersonal effectiveness. Do keep in mind, though, that human relations, the interactions between people, is a vast subject.

While you will learn communication skills specific to your work role in funeral service, my intent is not, nor should it be, to make you a therapist. After all, had you wanted to be a therapist, you would not have gone to mortuary science school. **However, it is highly probable that part of the reason you went to mortuary school was to be helpful to your fellow human beings. This training program will allow you to more effectively meet your need to be helpful to others.**

FORMAT OF TEXT

The material in this book has been ordered in a manner so that efficient learning will occur. The design is to present information sequentially with skills building one on another. Working from the front of the text to the back will be the most effective means of learning for the reader. This format will lend itself to learning for the novice, as well as the experienced funeral director.

Thanks to many funeral directors who have asked me to train their staffs, I have been able to refine the contents of this book over the period of several years. My initial training manual did not include the information outlined in Part IV. However, with encouragement of many of my funeral director friends, I have decided to include them in this more comprehensive text. Readers' comments and suggestions will, no doubt, prove helpful in decisions about what to include or exclude from any future editions.

While this book is designed to be used in a variety of ways, your participation in a **workshop setting with an experienced trainer is strongly recommended.** The opportunity to participate with others and to share experiences has proven to be an invaluable component of the training. Increased understanding typically comes from discussions, modeling, and group experiences, rather than from simply reading the text. Some value, however, would be gained by working through the book individually or in a small group.

This book is divided into five major sections consisting of twenty-three chapters. Part I recognizes the role of interpersonal skills in funeral service. Part II focuses on developing specific interpersonal skills and provides a sequential model of learning and practicing what you learn. Part III outlines potential barriers to effective communication. Part IV provides a comprehensive look at grief and mourning and Part V closes out the text with some important information about caring for you, the caregiver.

Activities have been included in an effort to assist you in looking at personal concerns, thoughts, and feelings related to your work in the area of interpersonal skills.

A CHALLENGE FROM THE AUTHOR

The time has come for those of you in funeral service to change how you manage and develop capable employees. Owners and managers need to make a strong commitment so that effective interpersonal skills and outstanding service are tied closely to business strategy. All too often, employee development is perceived as a narrow specialty rather than as a central part of mainstream business strategy.

Historically, people within funeral service have been slow to change. Too many owners and managers have treated the development of employee skills with aloofness, if not outright indifference. Employee training, particularly in the area of interpersonal skills and service objectives, has often been fragmented or nonexistent.

Hopefully, this is beginning to change. Wise owners and managers are beginning to see that mobilizing people toward service objectives is the way to create competitive advantage. Human performance results in service differentiation!

A key to successful funeral service practice is to translate customer needs (helpful interpersonal relationships and excellent service) into business objectives, and then to translate business objectives into employee performance requirements.

I once heard someone say, "Organizations don't do things. People do." Something terrific happens when you put effective interpersonal skills and excellent service at the top of your priorities. A number of other problems go away, because they are symptoms of not having the entire funeral home staff mobilized for results.

A bereaved family deserves the very best that you can provide in terms of service. Please remember—whether you are a receptionist, licensed director, student, part-time helper, manager, or owner—the family served is the one who is paying for everything and everyone. Yes, when you get people thinking about what matters to those you serve, you also get them thinking about how the funeral home earns its profit.

I challenge you to lead your funeral home staff in the direction of a total commitment to quality service. Leadership is about sharing a vision, setting objectives, creating opportunities, and moving forward. Funeral service seems full of people who manage, plan, and administer. But, they rarely move forward to lead a charge or champion a cause.

This cause relates to the existence of funeral service into the future. **I predict that unless families receive consistently outstanding service right now, funeral service as we know it will not exist in thirty years.**

REFERENCE

Raether, H.C., & Slater, R.C. (1975). *The funeral director and his role as counselor.* Milwaukee: National Funeral Directors Association.

CHAPTER 2

ACKNOWLEDGING THE NEED FOR INTERPERSONAL SKILLS IN THE FUNERAL HOME

"It is one of the most beautiful compensations of this life that no man can sincerely try to help another without helping himself."

Ralph Waldo Emerson

WHY BE A FUNERAL DIRECTOR?

One of the most frequent questions a funeral director is asked is, "What made you want to be a funeral director?" While as many answers can be given as there are funeral directors, a common theme often evolves from the content of the answer: **"Because I wanted to help people."** Helping others is an honorable involvement and, hopefully, you are proud to be a helping funeral director!

Helping a family before, during, and after a death is a very rewarding experience. Anyone who has ever helped a family during this time knows of the wonderful feelings that come from having helped. To learn how to help even more effectively will be even more rewarding.

The science and art of working in a funeral home requires a number of skills: business, technical, and interpersonal. **If we search for the difference that spells success for some and mediocrity or even failure for other funeral homes, the interpersonal area continues to surface as an important factor.**

Often, the routine parts of the job are relatively standardized from one funeral home to another, but the "personal" factor varies depending upon the desire, commitment, and patience of each and every funeral home employee who comes in contact with the family before, during, and after the funeral. The majority of your day as a funeral director is spent interacting with other people. As a result, your ability to skillfully develop and promote human relationships becomes very important. Keep in mind that these interpersonal skills are learnable, not inherent.

Most everyone knows when he or she talks with or observes others who have good interpersonal skills. They are persons we enjoy being around, both during times of work and play. The qualities and skills these persons possess are somewhat difficult to define because they represent a combination of skills. What makes sense, however, is that the helpful qualities we see in others are some of the same qualities we might want for ourselves. These helpful qualities and skills will be identified, explored, and illustrated in this book.

How often have you heard the comment, "The problem is poor communication?" The reality is that effective skills in interpersonal communication serve the foundation for successful living in this world. The American Institute for Research (Flanagan, 1978) worked to define the quality of life for Americans and evolved 15 categories grouped under five headings which are listed in Figure 2.1.

The significance of effective interpersonal skills is obvious as you review the list in Figure 2.1. One entire heading focuses on interpersonal activities **(RELATIONS WITH OTHER PEOPLE)** and the other four could not be fulfilled without good interpersonal skills.

PHYSICAL AND MATERIAL WELL-BEING

Material well-being and financial security

Health and personal safety

RELATIONS WITH OTHER PEOPLE

Relations with spouse (girlfriend, boyfriend)

Having and rearing children

Relations with parents, siblings, and other relatives

Relations with friends

SOCIAL, COMMUNITY, AND CIVIC ACTIVITIES

Activities related to helping or encouraging people

Activities related to local and national governments

PERSONAL DEVELOPMENT AND FULFILLMENT

Intellectual development

Personal understanding and planning

Occupational role (job)

Creativity and personal expression

RECREATION

Socializing

Passive and observational recreational activities

Active and participatory recreational activities (pg. 141)

Figure 2.1. Qualities of life as identified by American Institute for Research.

ESSENTIAL PERSONAL QUALITIES

When you think about the people in your circle of friends whom you most enjoy being around and then think about the personal qualities that they possess, what comes to mind? When given time to think about this question, most persons will mention some of the following qualities:

able and willing to listen,

trustworthy,

dependable,

understands me,

truthful with me,

will compromise,

sense of humor,

I feel comfortable with,

lets me be me, and/or

gives me permission to feel my feelings.

Add several of your own:

_____

_____

_____

As you review this list, one thing is obvious: **Interpersonal skills dominate the list.** This is important because we often think of education, training, job status, family background, and other noninterpersonal factors as being important in successful relationships, both business and personal. While true these factors can be beneficial, what really happens after you meet someone, regardless of who they or you are, is determined by the quality of your interpersonal relationship.

INTERPERSONAL SKILLS AND CHANGES WITHIN FUNERAL SERVICE

As funeral service continues to change and some funeral homes are being forced to close their doors, the interpersonal skills dimension in the profession will take on an even more important role. The need for effectiveness in interpersonal relationships extends beyond the funeral director to every funeral home employee.

As experience demonstrates, one negative interaction can cause headaches; that small incident can overshadow all of the good things that had been done before. This fact alone underlies the importance of skills training in interpersonal relationships for every funeral home employee.

Similarly, the person in the funeral home who answers the telephone, whether a secretary, part-time assistant, or student helper, frequently has the first contact with the family. Part-time help often interacts with family members to a large extent. These persons are on the front line, and an important aspect is for families to perceive them positively. The public's perception of anyone who is connected with the funeral home will be the very perception of the funeral home as a whole.

Historically, persons working within funeral service have been well-respected members of their communities. Funeral directors and other funeral home employees knew the families they served personally, and, as a result, the relationships were based on friendship through the years. This is still true in some locations. But in many areas, the increasing population, urbanization of formerly rural areas, expansion to the suburbs, and the frequent geographical distance between family members has significantly changed the families served. Add to these factors the general mobility of society; then the need for interpersonal skills training becomes even more apparent. As a result of public demand, the importance of interpersonal skills is rapidly moving from "desirable" to "necessary."

POTENTIAL ROLE CONFLICT BETWEEN HELPER AND BUSINESS PERSON

Directly related to interpersonal skill development in funeral service is the potential role conflict between helper and businessperson. I am often asked, **"Is it possible to be both a businessperson and a helper?"** **YES**. Anyone involved in helping professions must be a businessperson, or he or she will not survive very long.

The mix between helper and businessperson, however, has to exist so families will feel good about the service (thus, they must feel good about the staff). At the same time, the funeral home must be able to generate profit. The roles of helper and businessperson have to be in operation at the same time. Typically, if you provide good service, profits will follow. Consequently, service as a priority will generate successful business results.

One realistic goal for staff training in human relations skills is for all staff to possess the skills necessary to help people before, during, and after death, while maintaining a "helper" role in the eyes of the family. This is an achievable goal and one certain to lead to self-satisfaction and continued success of the funeral home.

INTERPERSONAL SKILLS TRAINING IS VITAL TO THE FUTURE OF FUNERAL SERVICE

In summary, human relations training is an essential ingredient for successful funeral practice. You obviously have a desire to enhance your skills or you would not be reading this material and participating in this training. So, relax, listen to yourself and others, participate, have fun, and most of all recognize that the development of self-confidence in interpersonal skills will prove to be a tremendous asset for yourself and the profession as well.

SUMMARY OUTCOMES OF CHAPTER

After reading and participating in the training related to this chapter you should (1) address why interpersonal skills training is essential to funeral service, (2) outline essential personal qualities you like your friends to have, (3) explore why all staff members in funeral homes should participate in this skills training, (4) acknowledge that it is possible to be both a businessperson and a helper, and (5) be able to begin to relax and enjoy this training experience! We have essentially set the groundwork for what lies ahead. Now lets have fun as we begin our journey toward even better interpersonal skills.

ACTIVITY 2.1
ROLE OF INTERPERSONAL SKILLS

Directions

In summary form, what is the role of interpersonal skills in your present position?

_____

_____

_____

_____

_____

_____

_____

_____

_____

_____

ACTIVITY 2.2
SENTENCE COMPLETION INVENTORY
REGARDING PERSONAL ATTITUDES
ABOUT BEING INVOLVED IN FUNERAL SERVICE

Directions

This sentence completion inventory is designed to help you begin to conceptualize, organize, and verbalize some of your thoughts and attitudes regarding your involvement in funeral service. Please complete each of the following incomplete sentences. There are no good or bad, right or wrong answers. Your responses can be used to generate a discussion in small break-out groups.

1. Being a funeral director is . . .

2. Helping people at the time of death . . .

3. Most young people think that funeral directors are . . .

4. When I think of my own death . . .

Activity 2.2 (Continued)

5. The best thing about being in funeral service . . .

_____

_____

_____

6. A funeral director should . . .

_____

_____

_____

7. I became involved in funeral service because . . .

_____

_____

_____

8. The most helpful thing I can do to help a family when they experience a death is . . .

_____

_____

_____

9. Those families which I most enjoy helping at a time of death are . . .

_____

_____

_____

10. Death is . . .

_____

_____

_____

Activity 2.2 (Continued)

11. When I speak with people on the telephone after the service . . .

_____

_____

_____

12. The worst thing about being involved in funeral service . . .

_____

_____

_____

13. When I see people on the street after I have helped them at a time of death, I . . .

_____

_____

_____

14. When I think of life in relationship to death I . . .

_____

_____

_____

15. My family thinks my involvement in funeral service . . .

_____

_____

_____

16. The time when I feel helpless related to my work in funeral service is when . . .

_____

_____

_____

Activity 2.2 (Continued)

17. Children who experience the death of their parents . . .

_____

_____

_____

18. A widow . . .

_____

_____

_____

19. The greatest need of the survivors after a death is . . .

_____

_____

_____

20. When the general public comes into the funeral home for tours . . .

_____

_____

_____

21. The future of funeral service . . .

_____

_____

_____

22. My first experience with death was . . .

_____

_____

_____

Activity 2.2 (Continued)

23. My ability to help people arrange for a meaningful funeral is determined by . . .

_____

_____

_____

24. Most old people think that funeral directors are . . .

_____

_____

_____

25. The day I decided to involve myself in funeral service . . .

_____

_____

_____

ACTIVITY 2.3
SELF-RATING INTERPERSONAL SKILLS

Directions

On the continuum line from low to high interpersonal skills place "S" for self, and "F" for majority of funeral directors you have had contact with.

X ————————————————————————— X

Low   High

REFERENCES

Flanagan, J.C. (1978). A research approach to improving our quality of life. *American Psychologist, 33,* 138-147.

CHAPTER **3**

CHARACTERISTICS OF THE HELPING FUNERAL DIRECTOR

"Look at people; recognize them, accept them as they are, without wanting to change them."

Helen Beginton

What personal characteristics make some funeral directors more helpful than others? We have probably all observed some funeral directors with bereaved family members who we can describe as being what we might term "natural helpers." What may seem natural are more probably characteristics and qualities that have been learned and developed over time. You, too, have the capacity to learn and make use of these helping qualities.

A general principle among people helpers is the following: **if you want to become more helpful to others, you must begin with yourself.** Our personalities form the basis upon which this helping process is built. The term "self as instrument" has been used in describing the person's essential helping tool as being oneself and acting spontaneously in response to the rapidly changing interpersonal demands of the helping relationship. In working with families following the death of someone loved, certainly rapidly changing interpersonal demands are placed on the funeral director.

We could review extensive research on personal characteristics of helpers. This would, however, probably leave us feeling overwhelmed, and we might begin to wonder if the "self-actualized" helping funeral director (those who have achieved self-understanding and fulfillment) exists out in the real world! As a consequence, our needs will be better served by expanding on those four qualities—empathy, respect, warmth and caring, and genuineness—most critical to the helping funeral director. However, for those of you wanting a more comprehensive review of general helper characteristics, a review is provided toward the end of this chapter.

To aid in the application of this material to your role as a helper within funeral service, make use of the activities at the conclusion of each characteristic. You then will be able to monitor yourself and receive feedback from others on whether you possess the characteristic described, whether it assists you in your helping efforts, or whether it needs continued work and refinement. Use the rating scale in Figure 3.1 to help you with this task.

HELPING CHARACTERISTICS

1. Empathy

Description: The ability to perceive another's experience and communicate that perception back to the person. As a helping funeral director, I listen to you as you speak to me, and though I cannot experience your experience, I begin to have a mental picture of the essence of what you are describing.

Discussion: Perhaps the most vital part of this characteristic is the ability to convey **accurate** empathy. Empathetic responsiveness requires the ability to go beyond factual detail and to become involved in the other person's feeling world, but always with the "as if" quality of taking another's role without personally experiencing what the other person experiences. If you experienced the same emotions as the person you are trying to help, you would be over involved. To have empathy for another person does not constitute the direct expression of one's own feelings, but rather focuses exclusively on the feelings expressed by another, and thereby conveys an understanding of them.

RATING YOUR PERSONAL CHARACTERISTICS
AS A HELPING FUNERAL DIRECTOR

A simple rating scale is provided here as a means to assist you in assessing the helping characteristics described in this chapter. Rate yourself on this scale now and from time to time as your growth as a helping funeral director continues. Ask your peers who observe you to rate you also.

CHARACTERISTICS DESCRIBED IN THIS CHAPTER	RATE YOURSELF FROM 1 TO 4
1. Empathy	_____
2. Respect	_____
3. Warmth and Caring	_____
4. Genuineness	_____

LEVELS OF HELPING CHARACTERISTICS

LEVEL 1 HARMFUL

(other person sorry they ever met you)

No evidence of characteristics present. Communicate the absence or lack of caring.

LEVEL 2 NEUTRAL OR INEFFECTIVE

(other person has difficulty trusting you)

Little, if any, evidence of characteristics present. Respond and communicate in a mechanical way.

LEVEL 3 HELPFUL

(other person finds you supportive)

Helping characteristics present most of the time. Clearly communicate caring and acceptance.

LEVEL 4 FACILITATIVE

(other person finds you to be encouraging, competent, and warm)

Helping characteristics consistently present in interactions. Your responses and attitudes convey empathy, respect, warmth and caring, and genuineness at all times.

Figure 3.1. Rating scale for personal characteristics.

The dimension of empathy is communicated when the family member feels the funeral home staff "understands." As you know, to say simply **"I understand how you feel"** is not enough. The dimension of empathy is communicated when the funeral home staff is able to respond at the emotional level with the family. The response goes beyond the "I understand how you feel" level to the ***"You really are feeling a sense of loss"*** level. In other words, empathy is communicated both verbally and nonverbally by understanding the person at the feeling or emotional level. You reach the family where they are right now, and the result is a feeling on their parts that you understand.

ACTIVITY 3.1
SELF-RATING ON EMPATHY

Directions

How do you rate yourself right now on the helping characteristic of empathy? _____ (Use Level 1 through 4)

Write any Notes or Questions you have on Empathy:

_____

_____

_____

_____

---

2. Respect

Description: The helping funeral director's ability to communicate his or her sincere belief that everyone possesses the inherent capacity and right to choose alternatives and make decisions.

Discussion: Respect requires a nonpossessive caring for and affirmation of another person, respecting another's right to be who and what they are. This quality involves a receptive attitude that embraces the other person's feelings, opinions, and uniqueness. The respectful, helping funeral director conveys a commitment to understand the person's feelings and opinions, even when those feelings and opinions are different than his or her own.

So, the dimension of respect is communicated when the family feels they have been allowed to make decisions without being pressured and when their opinions have been considered important. Respect grows out of an attitude on the part of the funeral home staff member that, "Other people know what is best for them better than I do." A sensitivity to other people which allows them to be themselves in a relationship will enable the family to feel that the funeral home staff respects them. Remembering what the person has said, demonstrating sensitivity and courtesy, and showing respect for the person's feelings and beliefs are the essences of communicating respect.

ACTIVITY 3.2
SELF-RATING ON RESPECT

Directions

How do you rate yourself right now in the helping characteristic of respect? _____ (Use Level 1 through 4)

Write any Notes or Questions you have on Respect:

_____

_____

_____

_____

---

3. Warmth and Caring

Description: The ability to be considerate and friendly as demonstrated by both verbal and nonverbal behaviors.

Discussion: Warmth and caring in the helping funeral director is demonstrated through a sense of personal closeness, as opposed to professional distance. Showing you are warm and caring is particularly helpful in the early phases of building a helping relationship. In addition, during a time of crisis (death obviously being such a time), the supportive value of warmth and caring is especially helpful.

The dimension of warmth is communicated primarily nonverbally. This is everything that influences the people around you other than the words used. For example, in the funeral home, touch is one of the most important nonverbal behaviors, though many others should be taken into consideration.

Warmth is a very powerful dimension in the helping process; in fact, when a discrepancy exists between verbal and nonverbal behavior, people almost always believe the nonverbal. A person's nonverbal behavior seldom lies. Consequently, a person who has excellent verbal communication skills, but lacks "warm" nonverbal behavior, would more than likely be perceived by the family as not helpful, indifferent, cold, uncaring, or some other negative label. As you will see in the chapter on attending skills, the warmth and caring dimension includes such things as eye contact, tone of voice, dress, physical distance, and gestures.

ACTIVITY 3.3
SELF-RATING ON WARMTH AND CARING

Directions

How do you rate yourself right now on the helping characteristic of warmth and caring? ___ (Use Level 1 through 4)

Write any Notes or Questions you have on Warmth and Caring:

_____

_____

_____

4. Genuineness

Description: The ability to present oneself sincerely. As a helping funeral director, this is your ability to be freely yourself — nonphoniness, nonrole-playing, nondefensive. It's when your outer words and behavior match your inner feelings.

Discussion: The dimension of genuineness involves disclosing how you feel about an issue. One important point to remember: try not to tell others how you feel too early. That is, your opinion may interfere with their ability to make a decision. How many times are you confronted by someone you don't know too well saying, "Here's what I think you should do . . . .," or "My impression is . . . .," or "You should'nt do . . . ." The point is that genuineness can be very helpful, but timing is important. The family's feelings should be explored first, followed by genuineness on the part of the funeral home staff. This is not to say that staff should be phoney, but rather they should be non-judgmental. This attitude will lead to a feeling by the family that the staff cares about them as individuals. You can earn the right to be genuine with others through first developing the relationship.

ACTIVITY 3.4
SELF-RATING ON GENUINENESS

Directions

How do you rate yourself right now on the helping characteristic of genuineness? _____ (Use Level 1 through 4)

Write any Notes or Questions you have on Genuineness:

_____

_____

_____

_____

A BRIEF REVIEW
OF HELPER CHARACTERISTICS

In reviewing the research on general helper characteristics, the following has been discovered.

Rogers (1958) believed that helpers must be open and the following conditions are necessary for helpee's (the person you are attempting to help) development in a helping relationship.

1. **Unconditional Positive Regard:** Helpers should communicate acceptance of helpees as worthwhile people, regardless of who they are or what they say or do.

2. **Congruence:** Helpers should demonstrate congruence between their sayings and behaviors. In other words, they should practice what they preach.

3. **Genuineness:** Helpers should be genuine and sincere, honest and clear.

4. **Empathy:** Helpers should be able to communicate empathetic understanding of helpee's frames of reference and should let them know they feel and understand the helpee's concerns.

Carkhuff and Truax (1967) developed Rogers' theoretical formulations into applied research and identified four core dimensions that facilitate effective helping relationships if communicated at high levels. They demonstrated that paraprofessionals as well as professionals can receive training to increase their levels of communication of these four dimensions. This increased communications ability has positive effects on the helpee's development and capacity to cope with life events. The dimensions are as follows:

1. **Empathy:** Helpers are able to communicate to the helpee their own self-awareness and understanding in relation to the helpee.

2. **Respect and Positive Regard:** Helpers can communicate their own warmth and caring.

3. **Genuineness:** Helpers can be honest with themselves and their helpees.

4. **Concreteness:** Helpers can be accurate, clear, specific, and immediate in their responses to helpee statements.

Combs et al. (1969) found in their research that effective helpers share certain beliefs about the following:

1. **Knowledge:** For effective helping to occur, helpers must be personally committed to specialized knowledge in their field and must find this knowledge personally meaningful.

2. **People:** People are viewed as able rather than unable, worthy rather than unworthy, internally rather than externally motivated, dependable rather than undependable, helped rather than hindered.

3. **Self-concept:** Helper's self-concept involves feeling personally adequate rather than inadequate, identifying with rather than apart from others, feeling trustworthy rather than untrustworthy, feeling wanted rather than unwanted, feeling worthy rather than unworthy.

4. **Helping Purposes:** Helpers are freeing rather than controlling people, deal with larger rather than smaller issues, are more self-revealing than self-concealing, are more involved with than alienated from helpees, are more process oriented than goal oriented in helping relationships.

5. **Approaches to Helping:** Helpers are more directed toward people than things, are more likely to approach helpees subjectively or phenomenologically than objectively or factually.

Brammer (1983) believed that the following characteristics are necessary in a helping relationship:

1. **Self-awareness:** Helpers should be aware of their own values and feelings, of the use (and power) of their ability to function as models for helpees.

2. **Interest:** Helpers should show interest in people and in social change.

3. **Ethical Behavior:** Helpers should demonstrate commitment to behaviors that are reflections of their own moral standards, of society's codes, and of the norms of the helping profession.

SUMMARY OUTCOMES OF CHAPTER

After reading and participating in the training related to this chapter you should (1) describe four personal characteristics essential to the "helping funeral director"; (2) rate yourself on each of these characteristics; and (3) be familiar with Rogers, Carkhuff and Turax, Combs, and Brammers theoretical and research-based essential helper characteristics.

REFERENCES

Brammer, L. (1983). *The helping relationship.* Englewood Cliffs, NJ: Prentice-Hall.

Carkhuff, R., & Truax, C. (1967). *Beyond counseling and therapy.* New York: Holt, Rinehart, & Winston.

Combs, A., et al. (1969). *Florida studies in the helping professions.* Gainesville: University of Florida Press.

Rogers, C. (1958). The characteristics of a helping relationship. *Personnel and Guidance Journal (37)* 6-16.

CHAPTER 4

UNDERSTANDING THE HELPING PROCESS

"Little happens in a relationship until the individuals learn to trust each other."

David W. Johnson

THE RELATIONSHIP

A major theme of this training material is that the development of an open, trusting relationship between the helping funeral director and those persons seeking assistance underlies any approach to the helping process. While developing a relationship can be time-consuming, a skilled helping funeral director can guide this development so the relationship can aid family members in a short period of time. Obviously, development of a trusting relationship becomes critical during the "at need" time immediately following the death of someone loved.

Development of a helping relationship begins with the initial contact with the bereaved family. As soon as communication between people has been established, relationships can develop. The relationship becomes the basis for meaningful contact between the helping funeral director and bereaved family members. People in crisis are typically open to the evolution of a helping relationship with persons who have the knowledge and ability to help them.

Through the context of the helping relationship, a climate is provided for people to explore their concerns and begin to make decisions about what will be helpful to them at this time. As the relationship grows between you, the helping funeral director, and the people who have turned to you for help, an opportunity exists to aid people in the process of self-exploration, self-understanding, and choices of action. Experience suggests building the relationship is critical to people experiencing the true value of the funeral experience.

PHASES IN THE HELPING RELATIONSHIP

A helping relationship can be visualized as having phases that help us understand how the process occurs. The seven phases outlined in this section of this book are typical of the helping funeral director after a death, but they do not always occur in this specific sequence, nor are all phases always present. The nature of how bereaved family members approach the helping relationship often helps determine the sequence and length of the phases. For example, some family members come with very specific requests, such as direct disposition of the body. Others wonder what their alternatives are as related to the funeral process. Obviously, these two examples demand a different kind of helping process. The diverse needs and desires of different families, therefore, call for some variation in these phases.

In a general sense, the following seven phases of the helping relationship may occur:

PHASE 1. Entering Into the Helping Relationship
A member of the family has phoned your funeral home and informed you of the death of a family member. The family member has asked for your assistance.

PHASE 2. Building a Helping Relationship
You respond by showing a willingness to assist the family. You offer counsel on what needs to be done now. You respond with concern and care to any questions they might have.

PHASE 3. Exploration and Assistance in Helping the Family Understand Their Alternatives

You listen and explore with the family the variety of alternatives available to them with regard to the funeral. You gather facts, explore feelings, and seek mutual understanding.

PHASE 4. Consolidation and Planning

You assist the family in coming to decisions about the funeral that best meets their needs. You jointly develop a specific action plan designed to best meet their emotional needs at this time.

PHASE 5. Implementation and Action

You conduct a funeral service that follows the planning model developed with the family. You bring together a variety of helping resources within your community to assist in this action-oriented helping process.

PHASE 6. Conclusion of the Funeral Process

You assist the family with a sense of closure upon completion of the funeral. You might join in the fellowship that often occurs following the completion of the funeral.

PHASE 7. Post-Funeral Service Follow-Up

After the funeral, you might have a structured follow-up program to offer additional assistance to families. You may serve as an informational and referral source for additional help-oriented services within your community.

Please note that the above sequence of general helping phases are designed to incorporate the following five factors:

1. development of the helping relationship,

2. exploration of alternatives related to the funeral,

3. enhanced understanding of the purposes for the decisions made,

4. development of a specific action plan, and

5. a provision for extended helping follow-up.

ACTIVITY 4.1
DISCUSSION OF PHASES
IN HELPING RELATIONSHIP

Directions

In small break-out groups, discuss the following questions.

1. Which particular phase outlined in this chapter is the easiest for you to carry out?

_____

_____

_____

2. Which particular phase outlined in this chapter is the most difficult for you to carry out?

_____

_____

_____

3. What is it like for you when a family doesn't seem to want a "relationship" with you, but instead they just want you to "carry out their wishes?"

_____

_____

_____

Activity 4.1 (Continued)

4. Do you think you consciously work to help the family feel good about the decisions they make regarding the "action-phase" of the funeral? If so, how do you do this? What do you do when you disagree with decisions the family makes?

_____

_____

_____

5. Do you currently have a structured post-funeral service follow-up program? If so, describe your program to other group members. What responsibilities do you think funeral directors have to families during the post-need period?

_____

_____

_____

SUMMARY OUTCOMES OF CHAPTER

After reading and participating in the training related to this chapter you should (1) describe why the development of a trusting relationship with the bereaved family is essential to the helping process, (2) outline and describe seven distinct phases in the helping relationships, and (3) name five factors that are incorporated into the sequential helping model outlined in this chapter.

PART II

DEVELOPING INTERPERSONAL SKILLS

CHAPTER 5

DEVELOPING ESSENTIAL HELPING SKILLS FOR SUCCESSFUL FUNERAL SERVICE PRACTICE

"Nature gave us one tongue and two ears so we could hear twice as much as we speak."

Epictetus

IS THIS AN "ART" OR A "SCIENCE"?

In many ways learning specific helping skills is like learning to paint on canvas. Even when certain skills or techniques are learned, the task is not accomplished. Why is that? Because once you as a funeral director learn a particular skill you must learn what it means to transcend the technique and develop the "art of helping."

So, another bias of this author is that helping our fellow human beings during times of crisis is every bit as much an "art" as a "science." Interpersonal skills are more than a collection of techniques. Helping others is a demanding interpersonal experience that requires energy, focus, and a desire to understand, not only other people, but oneself.

In essence, **understanding is the key to helping people create meaningful funeral rituals.** The capacity to communicate understanding and accurate empathy for bereaved people's experience is absolutely essential to becoming "artfully helpful."

Through effective interpersonal being and learning good communication skills you can gently enter into another person's world. Ultimately, the more effectively you communicate,the more helpful the relationship becomes in leaving the family feeling supported during this difficult time.

THE IMPORTANCE OF KNOWING YOURSELF

An old, but true statement reads as follows, "If you are going to help someone else, the place to start is with yourself." It seems that the more we know and understand about ourselves (our values, expectations, feelings, and reactions) the more we can understand and appreciate others.

Learning about your own perceptions of the world helps you come to understand others and their unique perceptions. As you explore yourself as a total person you hopefully allow and encourage yourself to grow and change. As you become comfortable with "who you are" others become comfortable being in your presence. In other words, self-acceptance and being at ease with yourself, helps others feel comfortable in your presence.

This self-growth attitude of continually striving to know who you are helps the families you serve come to trust you. The family will come to know who you really are as a person for you will have developed no need to hide behind a mask of being "Mr. or Mrs. Funeral Director." Obviously, what we are exploring here is being authentically who you are as a person.

To be authentic means to know and be yourself. Some people enter funeral service and discover early in the process that they "do not belong." In my experience this is often, not always, because they cannot be authentically who they are. Maybe they thought funeral directors all made tons of money and drove fancy cars. If this is what they valued and they couldn't achieve it quickly, they ended up leaving in search of these values elsewhere.

What I'm suggesting is that as we strive to know ourselves, understand ourselves, and accept ourselves, others will sense not only someone who possesses skills, but someone who also has a **compassionate presence.** If you do not discover this compassionate presence within yourself, you may well want to consider a different profession.

In summary, as you strive to know yourself, you become capable of "being present" with people in pain. You become capable of focusing outside of yourself on the needs of the bereaved family. You also become free to listen, to try to understand as much as possible, to attempt to understand what the family has been through and what they are going through right now.

So, knowing yourself also means not getting in the way of the people who come to you at a true time of need for support, understanding, and guidance. While you will never completely achieve total self-knowledge that results in being more "available" to others, only through making the effort can you approach it.

THREE LEVELS OF COMMUNICATION

Funeral director-family communication can be seen as an exchange between two or more people. And, actually, three very different, yet interdependent levels of communication exist.

The three levels we will identify and describe are

1. the exchange of information,

2. the exchange of emotion, and

3. the exchange of meaning.

The **exchange of information** involves the interaction of the funeral director obtaining essential factual information from the family, i.e., social security number, veterans information, etc. While this process may seem simple this exchange is complicated by the reality that humans do not give and receive information passively. The emotional state of each participant in the interaction, as well as how each person feels about each other affects the nature of the interaction. So, it's never as simple as just asking questions and getting answers.

Also an **exchange of emotion** occurs among participants. You are working with people in acute grief who will be very sensitive to your capacity to empathize and "be with" them. If the family senses interpersonal distance or a funeral director who just wants information so he or she can "get the job done," they will consciously or unconsciously pull away from the interaction. So, a constant awareness of people's "feelings" must be an integral part of the funeral director's helping role.

Finally, an **exchange of meaning** occurs. The family comes to you to create a funeral that will bring them meaning and purpose. As you communicate with them they "teach you" how you can help them create a meaningful funeral service. This means going beyond surface communication to seeking an understanding of how you can aid them in the "search for meaning." If they go away from the funeral without a sense of meaning or value, odds are they won't come back to you for service in the future.

The successful funeral director-family encounter consists of all three of these levels of communication. Awareness of these levels will allow you to stay conscious of how they impact your interactions with families served.

INTRODUCTION TO HELPING SKILLS TRAINING

To enhance your overall effectiveness as a helping funeral director, you must make use of communication skills involving perceiving nonverbal messages, hearing verbal messages, and responding verbally and nonverbally to these messages. To be certain that the skills outlined in this book become an integrated part of your tools as a helper, you must practice them frequently.

As you begin to learn these skills, you will probably find yourself concentrating more than ever before on your communication behaviors. This is certainly natural and may result in some initial feelings of discomfort and tension. With time, however, you will find yourself relaxing and discovering that the learning process is very rewarding. You will probably find yourself proceeding through four distinct phases in learning the helping skills taught in this section of the book. (See Figure 5.1.)

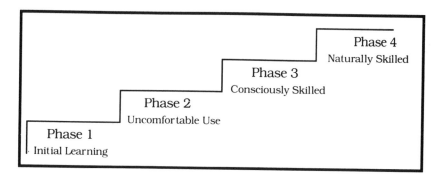

Figure 5.1. Progression of skill acquisition.

Understanding the following four phases of learning can make this training much more enjoyable. You can relax and not berate yourself when you don't immediately use the skill to the best of your ultimate capability. In other words, learning takes place over time and with focused practice.

PHASES OF ACQUIRING NEW INTERPERSONAL SKILLS

Phase 1. Initial Learning

This phase involves learning that some skills are available to you that you may not have known about. This may result in a combination of excitement about learning something new and some fear about the acquisition process. But again, remember, with appropriate training and practice you can acquire the ability to communicate even more effectively!

Phase 2. Uncomfortable Use

In this phase you have increased your awareness of some new ways of communicating but probably experience some difficulty in using the new skills. You may feel mechanical and like this really isn't you speaking or listening. You don't feel spontaneous because you have to think very carefully as you attempt to use any new skill.

Phase 3. Consciously Skilled

In this phase you begin to use the skills more effectively; however, you continue to be self-conscious as you use them. You are getting better at using the skills, but they still feel somewhat mechanical. You begin to use language that is natural to who you are.

Phase 4. Naturally Skilled

This final phase occurs only after you have completed the training and practiced the skills extensively. You must use the skills on a daily basis over an extended time to get to this level of skill. When you achieve this level, the skills come naturally and comfortably without you even consciously thinking about them.

Remember as you progress through these four phases of learning you will regress from time to time. But, don't give up! This regression is a normal part of any new learning experience. Keep envisioning yourself eventually interacting with people consistently at level four—and you will get there. Just keep in mind—**PRACTICE, PRACTICE, AND PRACTICE.**

In Chapters 6 through 14, specific helping skills are outlined so that you will learn specific human relations/communications skills in a sequential fashion. They focus on your ability as a funeral director to better understand yourself and others. These skills will be helpful from the initial point of contact with bereaved families, during the arrangement conference, as well as in the extended period of follow-up. An added bonus is that these skills will aid you in all of your interpersonal relationships with family, friends, and co-workers.

Once you have learned to make use of these skills, you will find the results rewarding. The people you have contacted will feel better understood and confirm this feeling in their interactions with you. After all, you can expect people to respond positively when they feel a sense of understanding from you.

Good luck as you work toward becoming an even more effective helping funeral director.

FORMAT FOR LEARNING HELPING SKILLS

Primarily for the purpose of learning in a workshop format, each skill to be learned has been described in a comprehensive eight-step procedure as follows:

1. define the skill,

2. identify purposes for using the skill,

3. enhance understanding of the skill,

4. illustrate its use,

5. identify outcome expected by helping funeral director,

6. role-play the skill with demonstration by trainer,

7. summarize and list guidelines for the skill, and

8. make notes or questions you have for the trainer related to this skill.

This model for teaching and learning has worked well in the training of numerous funeral directors. Reseach supports the value of this type of break-down approach to building skills. This instructional strategy divides a number of skills into teachable parts. With good teaching and appropriate practice you will eventually be able to put the various skills and their component parts together in a natural and helpful way.

Isn't it exciting to think about the new tools you will have available to you in your life's work?

CHAPTER 6

SKILL ONE: ATTENDING OR LISTENING

1. DEFINE THE SKILL

a. Attending or listening is when the funeral director physically communicates interest or gives attention to the person.*

b. The funeral director gives the person undivided attention; by means of verbal and nonverbal behavior; he or she expresses a commitment to focus completely on the person.

c. Listening is the focus—listening for verbal as well as nonverbal clues.

In your role as a helping funeral director, you are often called upon to help either people you are currently serving or people you have served in the past. Learning how to listen effectively is an excellent means of putting your care into action. As you know from your own experiences, people need to be listened to and they sense others understand them.

As a funeral director you may be, and often are, one of the very few people who really listens to grieving family members. Even when people are surrounded by family and friends, they

---

NOTE The word "person" is used throughout this book. However, the word "family" could also frequently be used since you may be helping a number of persons.

often are not really listened to. If you communicate your concern by being a good listener, you will have come a long way toward becoming a more effective and helping funeral director.

Personal Qualities of An Effective Listener

An effective listener has three personal qualities.

Desire. Perhaps the single most important characteristic of the good listener is desire. While this sounds simplistic, you need to want to listen. If you do not want to listen, chances are you will not listen. Through the process of listening you will be demonstrating your concern and acceptance of the person you are helping. Remember—people can quickly detect a superficial desire to listen.

Commitment. An effective listener not only needs to have a general desire to listen, but also needs to have a commitment to the task of listening. To be committed means to be responsible. If you are unable to talk at a particular time, be honest. Share your desire to talk and arrange for another time.

Patience. Combined with desire and commitment, the listening funeral director needs to have patience. Once you have made the decision to listen by involving yourself, take your time and patiently listen to the other person. If you are in a hurry and are anxious to get the situation "taken care of," chances are that you will do a poor job of listening. Keep in mind that the experience of grief will vary in intensity and length with different people. Be patient and available to provide the understanding they seek from you as an effective listener. People often know what they can and cannot do about thoughts and feelings they express; however, what they need are patient listening ears.

Related to the quality of patience is learning that you do not have to try to fill every silence during the listening experience. There is a time for speaking and a time for silence. Sometimes in your effort to help, you may feel the need to keep the conversation going. Discipline yourself and remember: Listening also involves listening to the silent moments as the other person struggles to express a feeling or pauses to consider a thought.

So, by keeping in mind the importance of the qualities of desire, commitment, and patience, you are well on your way to becoming an even more effective listener!

2. IDENTIFY PURPOSES FOR USING THE SKILL

a. Attending communicates to the person that you are giving your undivided attention.

b. It communicates that you are trying to understand what they are saying. You are **listening,** and that behavior makes them aware of your concern.

3. ENHANCE UNDERSTANDING OF THE SKILL

We will review the following major components that play a part in attending or listening behaviors.

a. Eye Contact	f. Setting
b. Posture	g. Voice Tone
c. Physical Distance	h. Rate of Speech
d. Facial Expression	i. Level of Energy
e. Gesture	j. Physical Appearance

One of the easiest things to do when communicating is to focus on the content of what the other person is telling you. You hear the words that are spoken, and respond to them. Unless you apply yourself, you can easily be unaware of the wealth of information people communicate to you in nonverbal ways. When you learn that more than two-thirds of all communication takes place through nonverbal means, you can understand the importance of developing attending skills.

Attending skills are the physical behaviors you use while listening to another person. These behaviors—eye contact, posture, physical distance, facial expression, the general setting— convey messages to the families you serve whenever you are with them. (See Figure 6.1.)

EFFECTIVE USE	NONVERBAL MODES OF COMMUNICATION	DESTRUCTIVE USE
These behaviors encourage expression of thoughts/feelings because they demonstrate mutual acceptance and respect.		These behaviors will probably stop or discourage conversation.
Maintains appropriate gaze; not a stare, but not looking away.	**EYE CONTACT**	Lack of contact; frequently shifts gaze, or stares.
Leans forward, relaxed yet attentive.	**POSTURE**	Stiff and rigid; leaning backward.
Natural distance; three feet, or approximately arms-length.	**PHYSICAL DISTANCE**	Very close; far away.
Matches emotional tone of situation; communicates empathy and warmth.	**FACIAL EXPRESSION**	Not congruent with emotional tone of situation; hides face behind hands.

Figure 6.1. Attending skills for funeral home staff.

Figure 6.1. Continued.

Casually draws people together; free from interruptions; pleasant colors; well-organized.	**SETTING**	Physical barriers; frequent distractions; dull colors; extremely formal or too casual; disorganized.
Seated in open position; nothing between self and other person(s); on same eye level.	**POSITION**	Barriers, like desk or table, are be-tween self and other person; self seated in dominant position.
Voice matches emotional tone of situation; relaxed; appropriate volume for hearing.	**VOICE TONE**	Does not match emotional tone of situation; too loud or too soft; sounds nervous.
Speaks at natural pace; at times, slower than usual.	**RATE OF SPEECH**	Too slow or too fast; indicates im-patience.
Are congruent with content; move slowly and appropriately; naturally; unobtrusively.	**GESTURES**	Tense, sudden movements; don't match content; compete for attention with words.
Toward	**MOVEMENT**	Away
Maintains alertness through lengthy arrangement conference or long interaction; appears to have energy appropriate to situation.	**LEVEL OF ENERGY**	Has difficulty maintaining con-centration; appears sleepy, uninterested; jumpy; pushy; lethargic.

Figure 6.1. Continued.

Responds to family at first opportunity; shares time with them; continues to respond appropriately.	TIME	Makes family wait; continues with what has been happening before responding.
Clean; well-kept; neat.	PHYSICAL APPEARANCE	Disheveled; lack of cleanliness.

Effective attending skills communicate that you are interested and concerned about the people you help at a time of death. If attending skills are ineffective, a helping relationship may not be established between you and those families you serve. This section will describe and assist you in developing attending skills as well as help you become more aware of the nonverbal communication of those around you.

No specific rules to follow are available in using attending skills. Some general principles, however, will help you use behaviors that are effective and avoid those that are ineffective. The guidelines for attending skills will allow you to express your uniqueness as a helping person when you are involved with people at a critical time in their lives. Also, keep in mind that cultural differences will influence the appropriate use of many of these components of attending.

Major Components of Attending

Now let's highlight several of the major components of attending.

Eye Contact. Perhaps the most effective way of making contact with people, especially shortly after a death, is through the use of your *eyes.* You attend to the person, or entire family, by looking at them and usually their eyes. This is a way of communicating your concern and interest in them; eyes are one of the key modes of communicating. While you certainly do not have to maintain a fixed stare, the appropriate procedure is to look at the people you are helping both while they are talking with you and during times of silence. Also, don't ignore people who by their nature or current emotional state are very quiet. You still want to make eye contact with them to help them feel included and supported.

Posture. A second component of attending is **posture.** Each moment of every day, we communicate a great deal by how we stand, sit, and walk. Take a moment right now to become aware of your posture and what it might communicate to someone entering the room. When you are involved in a helping relationship, your posture can communicate an interest and readiness to assist. Also helpful is communicating a sense of relaxation with your posture as it can have an important calming effect on the individual or family you are aiding. If you are tense, you will take the focus away from others and put it on yourself.

Physical Distance. A third component of attending is the **physical distance** between you and the people you are helping. At times, an appropriate behavior is to move in very close as you reach out to comfort. (At first, of course, this would be somewhat dependent on your relationship with the family.) Use the other person's reaction as a guide. If they pull away, take that as an indication that you are too close. We have found that most individuals and families are most comfortable at a distance of about three feet. You must take responsibility for seating yourself in the arrangement room, in the home, or other places in a position where you can communicate most effectively with all of those present.

Facial Expression. A fourth related component of attending is your **facial expression.** The expression on your face should match, as closely as possible, the emotional tone of what is occurring around you. Few people are more aware of the importance of this than those involved in funeral service. Your facial expressions can easily communicate a sense of warmth, as well as the message, *"I am with you, I understand, and I want to help you."* You may find that you communicate something differently with your facial expression than you are aware. After all, to see your facial expression is difficult unless you look in a mirror. You might want to ask your family, friends, and co-workers how they perceive your different facial expressions.

Setting. A fifth attending element is the *setting.* Of course, at times you have little, if any, control over the setting. Your initial contact with the family (excluding the telephone) may be in their home, the hospital, or a nursing home. Within the funeral home, however, you have an opportunity to create a setting that is most conducive to effective helping. The arrangement room should be a place that affords the family your undivided attention. Interruption and distractions should be eliminated as much as possible.

Furniture can be arranged in a way that draws people together, as opposed to spreading them out. Pleasant colors can be used for both the furniture and the walls. Desks or tables often hinder the communication process. By doing away with the desk, you may be able to involve yourself with the family and better communicate your openness. Research has found that some people like to sit at a round table (like in a kitchen) because they are used to discussing problems around a table.

Essentially, different families have different preferred settings for communicating, and you need to be able to offer choices and adapt to their unique needs.

Gesture. A sixth component of attending is *gesture.* You communicate much with your body movements. Your gestures should be natural and not interfere with your intended communication. If you move quickly or have mannerisms that are distracting, you will take a great deal away from your ability to help. Ask yourself if the messages you give with your gestures are those that you intend to communicate.

Other Components of Attending

In Figure 6.1 are listed a number of additional elements of communication and, in general terms, behaviors are described that may be either effective or destructive. You will want to review these different components of attending and **consider your own use of them with families you serve.**

Destructive attending behaviors tend to stop conversation or prohibit a helping relationship from being established. If you find yourself unable to attend effectively over a period of time, you will most likely notice some changes in the family's behavior. They may become passive and have difficulty in sharing their hurt in a mutual relationship. The result is that you'll probably move into a question/answer pattern difficult to get out of. On the other hand, they may become upset, impatient, and angry because you do not appear interested and concerned. These are signs that your attending skills are lacking and indicate that the person is not satisfied with the level of attention you are offering.

4. ILLUSTRATE USE OF ATTENDING

a. Trainer will illustrate this skill through demonstration because of the nonverbal component of the skill.

b. To aid in observing the illustration you are about to see, keep in mind: one easily recognizes when people are not listening; they are obviously engaged in another activity. Sometimes people also may be responding, but their nonverbal behavior says they are not with you. Be aware of what effect your attending has on people responding to you.

c. Trainer demonstrates this skill through structured role-play in front of group.

5. IDENTIFY OUTCOMES EXPECTED

a. Makes it easier for you as funeral home staff member to listen and remember, especially when the person you are helping is in the initial phases of grief.

b. Gives both you and the person you are getting to know an opportunity to get to know each other. Often the person you are helping is not only in an emotional phase of shock and numbness; he or she is looking for help from someone unknown.

c. Gives permission to the person you are helping to express himself or herself because you are giving fully of your own energy, time, and attention. This helps build a good base for a relationship.

d. Furthers the goal of allowing the person to self-explore. By allowing the person or family to talk about what is important, you gather a tremendous amount of information without asking specific questions.

e. Communicates that you are trying to understand. You are **listening** and aware of the person's concerns.

6.   ROLE-PLAY DEMONSTRATION

Trainer will do any additional role-play modeling to enhance the ease of learning for participants.

ACTIVITY 6.1
COMMUNICATING THROUGH ATTENDING SKILLS

Directions

Work in triads. One person (speaker) should talk freely for five minutes about any topic of interest. The second person (helper-listener) to whom he or she is speaking will listen, although he or she may ask questions or otherwise encourage the speaker to continue. The third person (observer-rater) will rate the helping funeral director (listener) on attending skills using the Observer's Guide for Attending Skills (Form 6.1).

Expectations

The person in the helper-listener role should be able to demonstrate consistent use, as judged by the trainer and observer-rater, of effective attending skills in a five minute interaction.

GENERAL GUIDELINES FOR PROVIDING FEEDBACK

"Feedback" in the context of this training is communication to a person for the purpose of providing to that person information about how he or she is progressing in the use of helping skills. Giving and receiving feedback is an excellent means of helping yourself and others refine the use of skills outlined in this manual. What follows are some specific guidelines to keep in mind when giving feedback to others.

1. Feedback is descriptive, not evaluative. By describing one's own reaction, it leaves the individual free to use that reaction or not use it as he or she sees fit. By avoiding evaluative language, it reduces the need for the individual to react defensively.

2. Feedback is specific, not general. To be told that tone is "dominating" will probably not be as useful as being told "just now when we were talking about how to help during the arrangement conference you did not listen to what others said and I felt forced to accept your arguments or face attack from you."

3. Feedback takes into account the needs of both the receiver and giver. Feedback can be destructive when it serves only our own needs and fails to consider the needs of the person on the receiving end.

4. Feedback is directed toward behavior about which the receiver can do something. Frustration is only increased when a person is reminded of some shortcoming over which he or she has no control.

5. Feedback is solicited, rather than imposed. Feedback is most useful when the receiver has formulated the kind of question which the observer can answer.

6. Feedback is well-timed. In general, feedback is most useful at the earliest opportunity after the given behavior (depending, of course, on the person's readiness to hear it, availability of support form others, etc.).

7. Feedback is checked to ensure clear communication. Have the receiver try to rephrase the feedback he or she has received to see if it corresponds to what the sender has in mind.

8. Feedback is checked with others in the group. Is this one person's impression or an impression shared by others? Both giver and receiver have a responsibility and obligation to check the accuracy of the feedback with others in the group.

7. SUMMARIZE AND LIST GUIDELINES FOR THE SKILL

_____

_____

_____

_____

_____

_____

_____

_____

_____

_____

_____

_____

_____

_____

_____

_____

_____

8. NOTES OR QUESTIONS YOU HAVE FOR THE TRAINER RELATED TO THIS SKILL

_____

_____

_____

_____

_____

_____

_____

_____

_____

_____

_____

_____

_____

_____

_____

FORM 6.1
OBSERVER'S GUIDE FOR ATTENDING SKILLS

Rate the following behaviors:
0 = did not occur
1 = occurred but needs improvement
2 = occurred adequately
3 = helper especially strong on this point

Nonverbal Behaviors

1. The helper maintained eye contact with the speaker.

$$0 \quad 1 \quad 2 \quad 3$$

Note: _____

2. The helper varied facial expressions during the interview.

$$0 \quad 1 \quad 2 \quad 3$$

Note: _____

3. The helper responded to the speaker with alertness and facial animation.

$$0 \quad 1 \quad 2 \quad 3$$

Note: _____

4. The helper sometimes nodded his or her head.

$$0 \quad 1 \quad 2 \quad 3$$

Note: _____

5. The helper had a relaxed body position.

$$0 \quad 1 \quad 2 \quad 3$$

Note: _____

6. The helper leaned toward the speaker to give encouragement.

0   1   2   3

Note: _____

7. The helper's voice pitch varied when talking.

0   1   2   3

Note: _____

8. The helper's voice was easily heard by the speaker.

0   1   2   3

Note: _____

9. Sometimes the helper used one-word comments such as "mm-mm" or "uh-uh" to encourage the speaker.

0   1   2   3

Note: _____

10. The helper communicated warmth, concern, and empathy through his or her facial expressions and other gestures.

0   1   2   3

Note: _____

CHAPTER 7

SKILL TWO: PARAPHRASING

1. DEFINE THE SKILL

a. Paraphrasing is a method of restating the person's basic message in similar, but usually fewer, words.

b. State in your words what the person has said.

c. Extract the essence of what the person has said.

2. IDENTIFY PURPOSES FOR USING THE SKILL

a. To allow you to test your own understanding of what the person has said.

b. To communicate to the person that you are trying to understand his or her basic message. You are **listening** to him or her, which makes the person aware of your concern.

3. ENHANCE UNDERSTANDING OF THE SKILL

Paraphrasing allows you to discriminate and respond to people without changing the meaning of what they have said. Again, the major purpose of paraphrasing is to be certain you understand what someone has said and to communicate that understanding back to them. This skill allows the person you are helping to expand on what he or she thinks and feels. The person will know that you are **really listening** when you accurately paraphrase.

You may find yourself tempted to "add to" the person's message. Try to overcome this urge. A real difference exists between paraphrasing and interpreting. If you find yourself adding to the person's basic message, odds are you have moved in the direction of interpreting or projecting your own thoughts into the interaction. This often takes the focus off the person you are helping and puts it on you.

To help yourself in the learning process, simply ask yourself, "What is this person saying and feeling?" Then, when a natural break occurs in the interaction, offer your paraphrase to the person. As you develop this skill you will discover that the person you are attending to will often confirm the accuracy of your paraphrase through verbal and nonverbal means.

Be patient with yourself and remember the learning phases involved in acquiring new skills. Learning how to accurately paraphrase will naturally take time to learn and require repeated experience with appropriate feedback from the trainer.

You will discover that paraphrasing dramatically enhances your ability to listen. To use this skill effectively, you must want to understand the person, to communicate meaningfully, and to relate with acceptance and trust. Your efforts to learn this and other skills outlined in this text are evidence of your commitment to enhancing your helpfulness as a funeral director.

4. ILLUSTRATE THE USE OF PARAPHRASING

Trainer will model this skill repeatedly to help participants in the learning process.

Illustration A

Bereaved Daughter: "The doctor was so helpful. He came by to see Mom every day and really seemed to care about her."

Funeral Director: "The doctor was a big help."

Illustration B

Bereaved Son: "Sometimes we would all be real serious. Then Dad would walk into the room, and everyone would brighten up. We would all laugh and carry on for hours at a time when he was around."

Funeral Director: "Your Dad could help people relax and have fun."

Illustration C

Bereaved Spouse: "My family really seems to know when I'm feeling sad about John's death. They encourage me to talk about what I'm feeling."

Funeral Director: "It sure sounds like you appreciate your family's concern for you."

5. IDENTIFY OUTCOME EXPECTED

a. The person experiences a feeling of being understood and accepted.

b. The person has a clearer perception of what they thought and felt.

c. The person has a sense of direction in the dialogue with you. The person is encouraged to continue to tell you more.

d. Paraphrasing quickly clears up any confusing communications. The person will occasionally correct you, but this simply aids in clarifying any misunderstanding of what you thought you heard him or her say.

e. Misperceptions are corrected before they increase to complete misunderstandings.

6.   ROLE-PLAY DEMONSTRATION

Trainer will do any additional role-play modeling to enhance the ease of learning for participants.

ACTIVITY 7.1
GROUP REHEARSAL WITH TRAINER PARAPHRASING

Directions

The trainer will talk to the group about any topic. The task is for everyone to **listen** and when a natural break occurs anyone can offer to paraphrase what the trainer has said.

Expectations

This will allow everyone to practice in the group setting in a non-threatening environment. The trainer will provide immediate feedback on the accuracy of the paraphrases and make any suggestions for improvement. This activity also allows participants to observe that paraphrasing often can occur accurately in more than one way. Participants will be encouraged to ask follow-up questions and clarify any misunderstandings related to this important skill.

ACTIVITY 7.2
TRIAD BREAK-OUT REHEARSAL
PARAPHRASING

Directions

Work in triads. One person (speaker) should talk freely for five minutes about any topic of interest. The second person (helper-listener) to whom he is speaking will concentrate on using the skill of paraphrasing. The third person (observer) will be available to provide follow-up feedback on the accuracy and helpfulness of the paraphrasing.

Each member of the triad will rotate through each of the three roles: speaker, helper-listener, and observer. The trainer will circulate throughout the room and be available for questions or concerns.

Expectations

Again, this activity will provide immediate feedback as participants work to develop this skill.

7. SUMMARIZE AND LIST
GUIDELINES FOR THE SKILL

_____

_____

_____

_____

_____

_____

_____

_____

_____

_____

_____

_____

_____

_____

_____

8. NOTES OR QUESTIONS YOU HAVE
FOR THE TRAINER RELATED TO THIS SKILL

_____

_____

_____

_____

_____

_____

_____

_____

_____

_____

_____

_____

CHAPTER 8

SKILL THREE: CLARIFYING

1. DEFINE THE SKILL

a. Clarifying is the process of bringing vague content in the interaction into clearer focus or understanding.

b. Clarifying goes beyond paraphrasing because you make a guess about the person's basic message and restate it.

2. IDENTIFY PURPOSES FOR USING THE SKILL

a. To allow you to clear up vague and confusing messages. In other words, it helps you make sense of what someone has said.

b. To enable both you and the person you are trying to help to have an increased understanding of what is being said.

c. To communicate to the person that you are trying to understand his or her basic message. You are listening; you are aware and concerned.

3. ENHANCE UNDERSTANDING
OF THE SKILL

When people are experiencing grief, communicating clearly becomes naturally difficult. The funeral director who learns to clarify skillfully can work to better understand the person through the use of this skill. When a person is in shock and disoriented he or she will usually have some trouble getting thoughts and feelings to flow from his or her head and heart.

The task of the funeral director becomes one of gently and artfully clarifying any confusing communication. Again, be careful not to interpret meaning, instead focus solely on clarifying. Be sure to state your clarifying remarks in terms of your own feelings of confusion, thereby avoiding any implications of criticism.

Again, remember that people experiencing grief are naturally confused. Also, keep in mind that the confusion might, in part, be due to your own inattention to what the person is saying. You can simply ask the person to restate what was said, ask for an example, or offer a paraphrase for the person to confirm your understanding. This skill will come with practice and you will probably find yourself using it more than you think.

4. ILLUSTRATE THE USE OF CLARIFYING

Illustration A

After a period of confusing discussion in which you have found difficulty understanding, you might say, "I'm confused, let me try to state what I think you were trying to help me understand." (You would then go on to attempt to paraphrase what you think the person was saying.) They would then either confirm or clarify any misperceptions you might have had.

Illustration B

After a period of confusing discussion that you have found difficult to understand, you might say, "I'm not real sure I understand, maybe we can go over this again." (You would simply slow down and review what was just discussed.)

Illustration C

After a period of confusing discussion that you have found difficult to understand, you might say, "I'm lost, could you tell me more?" (You encourage the person to expand on what he or she said to so as to assist you in understanding.)

5. IDENTIFY OUTCOMES EXPECTED

a. The result should be clearer statements and increased understanding on the part of the person you are attempting to help.

b. The person senses your attempt to help.

c. Clarifying encourages continued verbalization of thoughts and feelings.

6. ROLE-PLAY DEMONSTRATION

Trainer will do any additional role-play modeling to enhance the ease of learning for participants.

ACTIVITY 8.1
GROUP REHEARSAL WITH TRAINER
CLARIFYING

Directions

The trainer will talk in a rambling fashion to the group about any topic. The task is for everyone to **listen** and when a natural break occurs anyone can offer a statement of clarification.

Activity 8.1 (Continued)

Expectations

This will allow everyone to practice in the group setting in a non-threatening environment. The trainer will provide immediate feedback on the statement of clarification and make any suggestions for improvement. This activity also allows participants to observe that often more than one way is appropriate for seeking clarification. Participants will be encouraged to ask follow-up questions and clarify any mis-understanding related to this important skill.

ACTIVITY 8.2
TRIAD BREAK-OUT REHEARSAL
CLARIFYING

Directions

Work in triads. One person (speaker) should talk freely for five minutes about any topic of interest. The speaker will intentionally make some rambling statements that are difficult to understand. The second person (helper-listener) to whom he or she is speaking will concentrate on using the skill of clarifying. The third person (observer) will be available to provide follow-up feedback on the appropriateness of the statements of clarification.

Each member of the triad will rotate through each of the three roles: speaker, helper-listener, and observer. The trainer will circulate throughout the room and be available for questions or concerns.

Activity 8.2 (Continued)

Expectations

Again, this activity will provide immediate feedback as participants work to develop this skill.

7. SUMMARIZE AND LIST GUIDELINES FOR THE SKILL

_____
_____
_____
_____
_____
_____
_____
_____
_____
_____
_____
_____
_____
_____
_____
_____
_____
_____
_____

8. NOTES OR QUESTIONS YOU HAVE FOR THE TRAINER RELATED TO THE SKILL

_____

_____

_____

_____

_____

_____

_____

_____

_____

_____

_____

_____

_____

_____

CHAPTER 9

SKILL FOUR: PERCEPTION CHECKING

1. DEFINE THE SKILL

a. Perception checking is where you ask the person for verification of your understanding of what has been said over the past several statements.

b. Perception checking asks for feedback about the accuracy of your listening.

c. Checks that an understanding is taking place with the other person.

2. IDENTIFY PURPOSES FOR USING THE SKILL

a. To allow you to test your understanding of what has been said.

b. To provide an excellent method of giving and receiving feedback on the accuracy of the communication.

3. ENHANCE UNDERSTANDING OF PERCEPTION CHECKING

As previously noted, when people are in acute grief, frequently miscommunication occurs. Perception checking is a skill every funeral director should work to develop. Having the ability to ask supportively for feedback about your understanding of what is said will dramatically increase your overall interpersonal skills.

When you are in the position of helping others you should emphasize the importance of having clear and concise communication. The person you are assisting will appreciate your efforts to be certain that you are both understanding each other. Again, perception checking is an invaluable tool to use when working with people in grief.

4. ILLUSTRATE THE USE OF PERCEPTION CHECKING

Illustration A

"You expressed some doubt about using that particular minister. **Did I hear you correctly?**"

(Asking "Did I hear you correctly?" allows the person you are helping to clarify any confusion in your understanding.)

Illustration B

"**I want to check with you about what I think I heard you say.** You said you would like to have several family members participate in the service, but you don't want the service to be long?"

(Stating "I want to check with you about what I think I heard you say" helps the person realize that you want to check on your understanding.)

Illustration C

"While you would like to have music for the service, you are unsure you want organ music. **Is that right?**"

(Asking "Is that right?" allows the person you are helping to clear up any confusion in your understanding.)

5. IDENTIFY OUTCOMES EXPECTED

a. The person who you are helping experiences a feeling of being understood.

b. Perception checking is an excellent method of quickly clearing up any confusing communications.

c. It helps correct misperceptions before they become misunderstandings.

6. ROLE-PLAY DEMONSTRATION

Trainer will do any additional role-play modeling to enhance the ease of learning for participants.

ACTIVITY 9.1
GROUP REHEARSAL WITH TRAINER
PERCEPTION CHECKING

Directions

The trainer will talk to the group about any topic. The task is for everyone to **listen** and when a natural break occurs anyone can offer a perception-checking statement.

Expectations

This will allow everyone to practice in the group setting in a non-threatening environment. The trainer will provide immediate feedback on the perception check and make any suggestions for improvement. This activity also allows participants to observe that often more than one way is appropriate for doing perception checking. Participants will be encouraged to ask follow-up questions and clarify any misunderstandings related to this important skill.

ACTIVITY 9.2
TRIAD BREAK-OUT REHEARSAL
PERCEPTION CHECKING

Directions

Work in triads. One person (speaker) should talk freely for five minutes about any topic of interest. The second person (helper-listener) to whom he is speaking will concentrate on using the skill of perception checking. The third person (observer) will be available to provide follow-up feedback on the appropriateness of the statements of perception checking.

Each member of the triad will rotate through each of the three roles: speaker, helper-listener, and observer. The trainer will circulate throughout the room and be available for questions and concerns.

Expectations

Again, this will provide immediate feedback as participants work to develop this skill.

7. SUMMARIZE AND LIST GUIDELINES FOR THE SKILL

_____

_____

_____

_____

_____

_____

_____

_____

_____

_____

_____

_____

_____

_____

_____

8. NOTES OR QUESTIONS YOU HAVE
FOR THE TRAINER
RELATED TO THE SKILL

_____

_____

_____

_____

_____

_____

_____

_____

_____

_____

_____

_____

_____

_____

CHAPTER 10

SKILL FIVE: LEADING

1. DEFINE THE SKILL

a. Leading is anticipating where the person is going and responding with an appropriately encouraging remark.

b. Leading is the helping funeral director's impact on, or thinking ahead of, the person.

c. It is you slightly anticipating the person's direction of thought as a method of stimulating talk.

2. IDENTIFY PURPOSES FOR USING THE SKILL

a. To encourage the exploration of thoughts and feelings and to expand on the thoughts and feelings already discussed.

b. To allow the person freedom to explore in a variety of directions and to respond freely to what is occurring.

c. To encourage the person to actively retain a portion of the responsibility for direction of the interaction. In a sense, you are actually following his or her lead, while providing a sense of direction based on the content of what is expressed to you.

3. ENHANCE UNDERSTANDING OF LEADING

The skill of leading gives the person permission to "tell his or her story" or expand on what has been said. As you know, people will often have a need to explore events prior to the death of the person who has died. This process is healing and is encouraged by the effective use of leading.

Two different kinds of leading exist—indirect and direct. Let's take a moment to distinguish between the two.

Indirect leading often helps get the person started talking about whatever is important to him or her. Indirect leading is general in nature and allows the person to explore his or her own ideas and sense of direction.

Direct leading is where you focus the area to be discussed more specifically. This allows the person to expand on some important area that has been brought into the discussion. The illustrations that follow will clarify the distinctions between these two forms of leading.

Some people with whom you interact in a funeral director helping role will find that leading is encouraging. They will experience more responsibility for the content of what is being discussed. Other people find leading more threatening; they want you to do most of the talking, advising, and questioning. You can follow their leads as to how active a role to play in the discussions.

You must be careful, however, not to assume that they want to play a very minimal role. Many people become naturally passive as a part of the initial phases of the experience of grief. With supportive encouragement and the opportunity to become active, these very people are often capable of becoming an important part of discussions and the decision-making process.

4. ILLUSTRATE THE USE OF INDIRECT LEADING

Illustration A

"What else can you think of that might be helpful to talk about?" (Such statement allows the person to go in whatever direction he or she wishes.)

Illustration B

"Are there any questions you have of me before we get started?" (This statement allows the person to pose questions of most importance to him or her.)

Illustration C

Pausing and looking expectantly at the person can often serve as an indirect lead. (Your nonverbal message tells the person that you are willing to talk about whatever he or she wants.)

5. ILLUSTRATE THE USE OF DIRECT LEADING

(Again, remember that direct leading differs from indirect leading in that it helps focus the topic more specifically.)

Illustration A

"Could you tell me more about your mother's illness?" (This statement allows the person to teach you more about the nature of his or her mother's illness.)

Illustration B

"It sounds like the music is one of the most important parts of the service to you. Can you help me understand more about what kind of music you want?" (This statement encourages the person to expand on the music.)

Illustration C

"You mentioned that the holidays are the most difficult for you. Can you help me understand that?" (Such statements allow the person to tell you more about why the holidays are the most difficult for him or her.)

6. IDENTIFY OUTCOMES EXPECTED

a. The person whom you are helping experiences a sense of sharing the responsibility for the interaction.

b. The person is allowed to determine where he or she needs to go.

c. Leading frees you from feeling "over-responsible" for the total direction of the interaction.

7. ROLE-PLAY DEMONSTRATION

Trainer will do any additional role-play modeling to enhance the ease of learning for participants.

ACTIVITY 10.1
GROUP REHEARSAL WITH TRAINER
LEADING

Directions

The trainer will talk to the group about any topic. The task is for everyone to **listen** and when a natural break occurs anyone can offer a leading statement. Indirect leads will be concentrated on initially, then direct leads.

Expectations

This will allow everyone to practice in the group setting in a non-threatening environment. The trainer will provide immediate feedback on the leading and make any suggestions for improvement. This activity also

---

Activity 10.1 (Continued)

allows participants to observe that often more than one way is appropriate for leading. Participants will be encouraged to ask follow-up questions and clarify any misunderstanding related to this skill.

ACTIVITY 10.2
TRIAD BREAK-OUT REHEARSAL
LEADING

Directions

Work in triads. One person (speaker) should talk freely for five minutes about any topic of interest. The second person (helper-listener) to whom he is speaking will concentrate on using the skill of leading. Indirect leads can be practical initially, then direct leads. The third person (observer) will be available to provide follow-up feedback on the appropriateness of the leading statements.

Each member of the triad will rotate through each of the three roles: speaker, helper-listener, and observer. The trainer will circulate throughout the room and be available for questions and concerns.

Expectations

Again, this will provide immediate feedback as participants work to develop this skill.

8. SUMMARIZE AND LIST GUIDELINES
FOR THE SKILL

_____

_____

_____

— _____

_____

_____

_____

_____

_____

_____

_____

9. NOTES OR QUESTIONS YOU HAVE
FOR THE TRAINER
RELATED TO THE SKILL

_____

_____

_____

_____

_____

_____

_____

_____

_____

_____

_____

CHAPTER 11

SKILL SIX: QUESTIONING

1. DEFINE THE SKILL

Questioning is a method for gaining information and increasing understanding.

2. IDENTIFY PURPOSES FOR USING THE SKILL

a. To gain information so you can assist the person with his or her concerns. Often the question will enable you to gain information for aiding the entire family during the arrangement conference.

b. To be able to question effectively increases understanding for both you and the person(s) you are helping.

Special Note

As a good general rule, question for only two purposes:

to obtain specific information, and

to direct the person's interaction with you into more helpful areas.

3. ENHANCE UNDERSTANDING OF QUESTIONING

Questioning is one of the most important helping skills for funeral directors. Both the funeral director and the family use questions to obtain information to clarify and to explore feelings and thoughts. We will discuss only a few of its many features for the purpose of this training.

Open-ended Questions

In the majority of instances, leading or open questions, rather than closed or pointed questions, are preferable. When you use leading questions, the person has a tendency to talk freely; you will unknowingly avoid putting answers in his or her mouth.

Open-ended questions encourage self-exploration. They are intentionally broad in nature and give the person freedom to determine the amount and kinds of information to give. In developing the ability to "artfully" use open-ended questions, the helping funeral director also communicates a willingness to assist in explorations of any content anyone wants to discuss.

Be aware that open-ended questions help:

a. ***Allow the person to tell more about what he or she might be thinking or feeling.*** For example ask, "Could you tell me more about that?"

b. ***Help the person better understand.*** Ask the question, "What do you think about music being played at the service?" as opposed to "Do you want to have music at the service?"

c. ***Focus on the feelings of the person.*** This concept is demonstrated when you ask, "How do you feel about having the casket open or closed?" as opposed to "Do you want the casket open or closed?"

Closed Questions

A closed question often emphasizes factual content as opposed to feelings. The use of too many closed questions can sometimes demonstrate a lack of interest in the process of creating a meaningful funeral for the family. People can tell if the funeral director just wants to "get the information to do the job" versus a genuine attempt to understand the needs of the family and create a meaningful funeral.

This is not to say that closed questions never have a place. Obtaining such information as date of birth and social security number are natural closed questions. Just be certain not to ask too many questions in a row that require only a yes or no answer, a specific recall, or a short one or two word answer.

Keep in mind that if you begin an interaction by asking closed questions and getting more answers you often set a pattern that is difficult to break. By initiating this pattern, you will be communicating that you have the responsibility for asking questions, and the person with whom you are talking is to answer them.

In effect, the person becomes an object, an object that answers when asked questions and otherwise, keeps quiet. By starting the question-answer patterns, you are plainly telling the person that you are the authority, the one in charge, and that only you know what is important. If you do think you are the only one that knows what is important, you might want to consider another vocation because as a funeral director you will find yourself getting disappointed and frustrated quite often.

Questioning Behavior

One other important note. When using questioning behavior, it's also critical to adjust your pace to that of the person. Going too slowly can suggest a lack of interest or understanding. Going too fast, however, is to miss important areas necessary to explore.

Going too fast also can be very confusing and disorienting to a person in grief. In a subtle way, it also says you are not really interested. Also, please remember not to push anyone to reveal more than he or she is ready to reveal at any time. The ability to first establish the relationship will allow for movement into areas which are difficult or painful to discuss. Obviously, knowing when to ask questions and how to pose them effectively is a vital skill for the funeral director.

In using questioning, be concerned about the readiness of the other person for questions and for the specific kind of questions—open-ended or closed. The following are reminders when questioning:

a. be aware that you are asking questions,

b. carefully weigh the content of the questions you do ask,

c. evaluate the need to ask questions,

d. examine the different types of questions available to you, and

e. become sensitive to the questions asked of you, whether asked directly or indirectly.

4. ILLUSTRATE THE USE OF QUESTIONING

(Keep in mind that open-ended questions are preferable when possible.)

Illustration A

Closed-ended: "How long was your dad sick?" (This question requires only a simple response, does not build relationship or allow the person to teach you about his or her experience.)

Open-ended: "Could you tell me a little bit about your dad's illness?"

Illustration B

Closed-ended: "Do you want to receive friends at the funeral home?"

Open-ended: "What do you think about receiving friends at the funeral home?"

Illustration C

Closed-ended: "Do you remember some good times?"

Open-ended: "What are some of the times you remember best?"

5. IDENTIFY OUTCOMES EXPECTED

By using open-ended questions when appropriate, you should be able to

a. help the other person become more trusting and open with you,

b. gather information without seeming to demand it,

c. create a helping relationship based on respect,

d. help maintain a meaningful conversation,

e. begin a conversation that will be continued by the other person, and

f. gain an increased understanding both for yourself and the other person.

6. ROLE-PLAY DEMONSTRATION

Trainer will do any additional role-play modeling to enhance the ease of learning for participants.

ACTIVITY 11.1
GROUP REHEARSAL WITH TRAINER
QUESTIONING

Directions

The trainer will invite the group to ask him or her questions. The task is for everyone to practice asking open-ended questions.

Activity 11.1 (Continued)
Expectations

This will allow everyone to practice in the group setting in a non-threatening environment. The trainer will provide immediate feedback on the questions and make any suggestions for improvement. This activity also allows participants to observe that many ways are available to gather information without seeming to demand it. In addition, a list of common areas where questions are asked in arrangement conferences will be reviewed. Participants will be encouraged to ask follow-up questions and clarify any misunderstanding related to this skill.

ACTIVITY 11.2
TRIAD BREAK-OUT REHEARSAL
QUESTIONS

Directions

Work in triads. One person (speaker) should talk freely for five minutes about any topic of interest. The second person (helper-listener) to whom he or she is speaking will concentrate on using the skill of questioning. The third person (observer) will be available to provide follow-up feedback on the appropriateness of the questioning.

Each member will rotate through each of the three roles: speaker, helper-listener, and observer. The trainer will circulate throughout the room and be available for questions and concerns.

Expectations

Again, this will provide immediate feedback as participants work to develop this skill.

7. SUMMARIZE AND LIST GUIDELINES FOR THE SKILL

_____
_____
_____
_____
_____
_____
_____
_____
_____
_____
_____

8. NOTES OR QUESTIONS YOU HAVE FOR THE TRAINER RELATED TO THE SKILL

_____
_____
_____
_____
_____
_____
_____
_____
_____
_____
_____
_____
_____

CHAPTER 12

SKILL SEVEN: REFLECTING FEELINGS

1. DEFINE THE SKILL

a. Reflecting feelings is when you express in fresh words the essential feelings, stated or strongly implied, of the person.

b. Expresses in fewer and different words the essential feelings that have been expressed.

2. IDENTIFY PURPOSES FOR USING THE SKILL

a. To communicate an understanding of what the person is feeling.

b. To communicate to the person that "I am hearing you," "I am with you," and "I am trying to learn from you — what you are feeling."

c. To help the person bring vaguely expressed feelings into clearer awareness.

d. To understand, as a helping funeral director, what the person is experiencing.

3. ENHANCE UNDERSTANDING OF REFLECTING FEELINGS

Working in funeral service means working with people who experience a wide range of feelings. Having sensitivity to whatever those feelings are is essential to successfully serving the bereaved family. During times of grief, emotional states override cognitive thought processes. This emotional overflow is signified by such phrases as "overwhelmed with grief."

Any effective interpersonal relationship requires the ability to be perceptive of what someone else feels. Emotional responses to others often determine whether we find them helpful, particularly during times of distress.

Bereaved persons vary in their emotional expressions. One person may openly express explosive emotions, confusion, or relief, while another may be unexpressive, numb, or in total shock. The helping funeral director must learn how to be respectful of whatever the person might feel.

Conveying an accurate understanding of what the bereaved person feels requires a desire to understand. Obviously, a desire to understand is a prerequisite to helping create a meaningful funeral service. Before learning how to reflect feelings, let's review some general information about feelings:

a. feelings are neither good nor bad, they just are;

b. everyone has a right to his or her feelings;

c. feelings always make sense when considered in context of the person's individual outlook on the world;

d. feelings are not dangerous (actions can potentially be dangerous); and

e. denying a feeling does not make it go away.

Having an awareness of the preceding information about feelings allows the helping funeral director to avoid any of the following actions:

a. denying the existence or importance of the person's feelings,

b. trying to suppress the person's expression of feelings, or

c. implying that something is wrong with the person's feelings.

Obviously, any such actions not only would detract from the funeral director's ability to help but also would give the message that something is wrong with the person being helped.

4. ILLUSTRATE THE USE OF REFLECTING FEELINGS

Illustration A

Bereaved Widow: "Right now, I really don't know what to do."

Funeral Director: "Sounds like you're feeling confused."

Illustration B

Bereaved Son: "The words that the pastor used during the service had so much meaning and purpose for me."

Funeral Director: "When you think about the message the pastor gave, you feel comfort."

Illustration C

Bereaved Widower: "She had been ill for so long. It's been so hard on everyone. I'm just glad she's out of her pain."

Funeral Director: "Sounds as if you feel relieved she doesn't have to go through all that anymore."

5. IDENTIFY OUTCOMES EXPECTED

a. Those persons you are helping will view you as one who understands what they are experiencing.

b. The person you are helping will be able to identify and express feelings more effectively.

c. The person you are helping will be encouraged to continue verbalizing thoughts and feelings.

Objectives Being Accomplished

When you, the helping funeral director, focus on how someone feels, you are responding in a helpful manner. By doing so, you are accomplishing one or more of the following objectives:

a. showing the person that you understand what he or she is experiencing;

b. supporting his or her feelings and, thus, supporting him or her;

c. helping the person focus in on his or her feelings;

d. giving the person the message that you accept his or her feelings.

6. ROLE-PLAY DEMONSTRATION

Trainer will do any additional role-play modeling to enhance the ease of learning for participants.

ACTIVITY 12.1
GROUP REHEARSAL WITH TRAINER
REFLECTING FEELINGS
Directions

The trainer will talk to the group about any topic. The task is for everyone to listen and when a natural break occurs anyone can offer to reflect a feeling.

Activity 12.1 (Continued)

Expectations

This will allow everyone to practice in the group setting in a non-threatening environment. The trainer will provide immediate feedback on the reflecting of feelings and make any suggestions for improvement. This activity also allows participants to learn that a variety of ways exist to reflect feelings appropriately. Special attention will be given to different ways to lead into reflecting feelings. Participants will be encouraged to ask follow-up questions and clarify any misunderstandings related to this skill.

ACTIVITY 12.2
TRIAD BREAK-OUT REHEARSAL
REFLECTING FEELINGS

Directions

Work in triads. One person (speaker) should talk freely for five minutes about any topic of interest. (Be certain to talk about something that generates feelings in you.) The second person (helper-listener) to whom he or she is speaking will concentrate on using the skill of reflecting feelings. The third person will be available to provide follow-up feedback on the appropriateness of the leading statements.

Each member of the triad will rotate through each of the three roles: speaker, helper-listener, and observer. The trainer will circulate throughout the room and be available for questions and concerns.

Expectations

Again, this will provide immediate work to develop this skill.

7. SUMMARIZE AND LIST GUIDELINES FOR THE SKILL

_____

_____

_____

_____

_____

_____

_____

_____

_____

_____

8. NOTES OR QUESTIONS YOU HAVE FOR THE TRAINER RELATED TO THE SKILL

_____

_____

_____

_____

_____

_____

_____

_____

_____

_____

CHAPTER 13

SKILL EIGHT: INFORMING

1. DEFINE THE SKILL

a. Informing is sharing of facts possessed by the funeral director.

b. Informing is providing information that will allow the person to make an informed decision.

2. IDENTIFY PURPOSES FOR USING THE SKILL

a. To convey the information through informing frequently which cannot be conveyed by any other means.

b. To enable the funeral director to communicate knowledge of customs related to death which is often a critical reason why people seek assistance.

c. To provide the information that allows people to make informed choices or to clarify decision processes.

3. ENHANCE UNDERSTANDING OF INFORMING

Informing people is an integral part of the funeral director's helping role. Providing information, or informing people, is usually a simple task; however, different ways of conveying information are possible, some of which are more helpful than others. The information must be usable to the person receiving it.

In addition, the person receiving the information must be willing to hear and apply what you have shared. The chance is good that the information was provided in an ineffective manner if the funeral director is ever labeled as "pushy," "a know-it-all," or "patronizing."

Some informing occurs in response to basic questions that the person might ask. For example, "Can you find a minister for us?"; "What are typical times that a family might receive people here at the funeral home?"; or, "Can you help us in arranging for some flowers?" The funeral director then informs the person in response to these questions.

Also at times you will need to provide information that the person may not have requested. This relates to people wanting to know "why?" you are telling them something. For example, you might inform a person that you are going to gather some information necessary for the death certificate. The fact that the funeral director informs them "why?" he or she must ask certain questions may not seem important at the moment, however doing so typically helps the person to be more tolerant of these questions. What other examples can you think of where informing people would be helpful?

4. ILLUSTRATE THE USE OF INFORMING

(Examples of ways to lead to informing are as follows.)

Illustration A

"I think you might find it helpful to be aware of some of the major differences between these caskets. Let me tell you about them..."

Illustration B

"This book has some different examples of what some people choose to do for flower arrangements. Maybe you would like to look through this as a family, and then I can answer any questions you might have." (In responding to any questions you become involved in information giving.)

Illustration C

"Are there any questions I can answer for you at this time?" (In responding to any questions, you become involved in information giving.)

5. IDENTIFY OUTCOMES EXPECTED

a. Persons will realize that you are interested in providing them with pertinent information to help them make decisions.

b. The person enables you to convey information within your area of expertise that someone needs at a particular time.

c. The person will hopefully perceive your informing as genuine attempts to be helpful.

6. ROLE-PLAY DEMONSTRATION

Trainer will do any additional role-play modeling to enhance the ease of learning for participants.

ACTIVITY 13.1
GROUP REHEARSAL WITH TRAINER
INFORMING

Directions

The trainer will sit quietly in front of the group. Each person in the group will be given the opportunity to offer an informative statement. The trainer may ask some participants questions in an effort to have them respond with informative statements.

Activity 13.1 (continued)

Expectations

This will allow everyone to practice in the group setting in a nonthreatening environment. The trainer will provide immediate feedback on the leading and make any suggestions for improvement. This activity also allows participants to observe that often more than one way is appropriate for using the skill of informing. A special discussion of the importance of **timing** and **pacing** the use of this skill will be included in the discussion. Participants will be encouraged to ask follow-up questions and clarify any misunderstanding related to this skill.

ACTIVITY 13.2
TRIAD BREAK-OUT REHEARSAL
INFORMING

Directions

Work in triads. One person (speaker) will pose natural questions that people often ask related to funeral service. The second person (helper-listener) to whom he or she is speaking will concentrate on using the skill of informing. The third person (observer) will be available to provide follow-up feedback on the appropriateness of the leading statements.

Each member of the triad will rotate through each of the three roles: speaker, helper-listener, and observer. The trainer will circulate throughout the room and be available for questions and concerns.

Expectations

Again, this will provide immediate feedback as participants work to develop this skill.

7. SUMMARIZE AND LIST GUIDELINES FOR THE SKILL

_____
_____
_____
_____
_____
_____
_____
_____
_____
_____
_____

8. NOTES OR QUESTIONS YOU HAVE FOR THE TRAINER RELATED TO THE SKILL

_____
_____
_____
_____
_____
_____
_____
_____
_____
_____
_____

CHAPTER 14

SKILL NINE: SUMMARIZING

1. DEFINE THE SKILL

Summarizing is a method of tying together several ideas and feelings at the end of a period of discussion or the arrangement conference.

2. IDENTIFY PURPOSES FOR USING THE SKILL

a. To increase understanding for both you, the funeral director, and the person.

b. To provide you and the person with a sense of having made progress.

c. To provide an opportunity for additional clarification whenever necessary.

3. ENHANCE UNDERSTANDING OF SUMMARIZING

Effective use of the skill of summarizing will prove to be a real asset to the funeral director. Summarizing helps the person realize that you have really focused in on what has been said. It is an excellent way to check on the accuracy of what has been decided and feelings that have been shared. In addition, summarizing is a natural way to make transitions from one content area to another, or, to simply conclude an interaction.

During stressful times people usually want a clear understanding of their situation and what decisions they have made. Refining your use of the skill of summarizing will help you better accomplish this sense of increased understanding and awareness. As you probably realize, when someone else summarizes decisions you have made or concerns you have, it often gives you an increased understanding of the situation.

During an arrangement conference, many ideas, thoughts, and feelings are shared. Experience suggests that to summarize effectively, you must be very attentive to the family. Being able to hear, understand, and remember important thoughts and feelings over extended time will allow you to restate in summary their most important concerns and reinforce decisions they have made.

Summarizing is particularly important because what occurs at the end of an interaction often determines a person's impression of you. Summarizing should be done at a pace that allows people to correct any misperceptions along the way. Some funeral directors may choose to write major points in the form of a summary and give this to the person. This written summary often includes such information as when the family will come into the funeral home for any private time, calling hours, service time, etc. With practice summarizing will become an integrated skill that is used frequently in your continued efforts to help people at a difficult time.

4. ILLUSTRATE THE USE OF SUMMARIZING

Examples of ways to lead naturally into summarizing are provided in the following illustrations.

Illustration A

"Maybe we would all find it helpful to review what we have talked about . . ."

Illustration B

"I'd like to take a minute to just go over everything you have decided . . ."

Illustration C

"Let's summarize what you as a family have decided will best meet your needs..."

5. IDENTIFY OUTCOMES EXPECTED

a. Summarizing reassures that you have heard what someone has said.

b. It allows persons an increased understanding and awareness of decisions they have made.

c. It is an excellent way of clearing up any confusion.

d. It is a natural way to conclude an interaction or make a transition into another area of discussion.

e. It provides people with a sense of movement, direction, and purpose.

6. ROLE-PLAY DEMONSTRATION

Trainer will do any additional role-play modeling to enhance the ease of learning for participants.

ACTIVITY 14.1
GROUP REHEARSAL WITH TRAINER
SUMMARIZING

Directions

The trainer will talk to the group for approximately ten minutes. The content will relate to some recent

---

Activity 14.1 (Continued)

decision-making process. Upon conclusion of the trainer's statements anyone can offer to summarize what was said.

Expectations

This will allow everyone to practice in the group setting in a nonthreatening environment. The trainer will provide immediate feedback on the summarizing and make any suggestions for improvement. This activity also allows participants to observe different styles of summarizing. Participants will be encouraged to ask follow-up questions and clarify any misunderstandings related to this skill.

ACTIVITY 14.2
TRIAD BREAK-OUT REHEARSAL
SUMMARIZING

Directions

Work in triads. One person (speaker) should talk for approximately ten minutes about some recent decision-making process. The second person (helper-listener) to whom he or she is speaking will concentrate on using the skill of summarizing. The third person (observer) will be available to provide follow-up feedback on the effectiveness of the summarizing statements.

Each member of the triad will rotate through each of the three roles: speaker, helper-listener, and observer. The trainer will circulate throughout the room and be available for questions and concerns.

Expectations

Again, this will provide immediate feedback as participants work to develop this skill.

7. SUMMARIZE AND LIST GUIDELINES
FOR THE SKILL

_____

_____

_____

_____

_____

_____

_____

_____

_____

_____

_____

8. NOTES OR QUESTIONS
YOU HAVE FOR THE TRAINER
RELATED TO THE SKILL

_____

_____

_____

_____

_____

_____

_____

_____

_____

_____

_____

_____

SUMMARY OUTCOMES OF PART II

After reading and participating in the activities related to Part II, Developing Interpersonal Skills, you should be able to (1) demonstrate an awareness of nine essential helping skills for the funeral director, (2) recognize the purpose for using a specific skill, (3) illustrate the use of these nine skills, and (4) be aware of summary guidelines related to each skill.

PART III

OVERCOMING
BARRIERS
TO
IMPLEMENTATION

CHAPTER 15

BARRIERS TO EFFECTIVE COMMUNICATION

"Communication is something so simple and difficult that we can never put it in simple words"

T. S. Matthews

A critical component of enhancing funeral director helping skills is an increased awareness of potential destructive communication patterns. The information and activities in this chapter will assist you in recognizing specific forms of destructive communication, thus allowing you to avoid them in your work. The patterns outlined include the following:

1. Funeral Director Dominance,

2. Bombarding with Questions,

3. Inappropriate Self-disclosure,

4. Offering Platitudes or False Reassurance,

5. Discouraging the Expression of Emotions and Tears,

6. Emotional Distancing.

FUNERAL DIRECTOR DOMINANCE

Dominating an interaction with another person can best be described by the following: general sense of impatience, changing the subject, attempting to persuade or coerce, and lecturing or preaching.

The "dominator" often thinks he or she knows the answer before the question is even posed. He or she thinks he or she knows exactly what people should do and likes to tell them when and how to do it. This person is often a very poor listener. Dominating behaviors communicate a sense of disrespect for a person's ability to decide what is best for his or her self. In Chapter 3, respect was noted as being one of the critical characteristics of the helping funeral director.

BOMBARDING WITH QUESTIONS

We have already discussed (see Chapter 11) how the excessive use of questions tends to limit the interaction. Relying largely on questions to gain information and understand feelings is destructive in that you, as opposed to the person you are helping, become the major focus in what is perceived as important.

The "bombarder" might run off a series of questions like, "What was your father's date of birth? Where was he born? What was his social security number? Was he a veteran?" This approach usually makes the person feel like an object instead of a person.

Bombarding with questions communicates that the funeral director is interested in facts, not feelings. In addition, this pattern of interaction is usually difficult to change. For example, if early in the relationship you assume a strong directive role characterized by excessive questioning, the person may consider this the expected situation and adopt a passive role.

INAPPROPRIATE SELF-DISCLOSURE

The "self-discloser" has been known to bore people to death. He or she likes to talk about self, particularly personal experiences. This person might say something like, "When my grandfather died we decided it would be best to . . ."

Remember that talking at length about oneself draws the focus away from the one you are attempting to help. Chances are slim that the person will find this of relevance to his or her own situation.

Self-disclosure on your part can be appropriate on occasion; however, in general, the best procedure is to keep the focus of your helping efforts on those you are assisting. What are some occasions when you think self-disclosure might be appropriate?

OFFERING PLATITUDES OR FALSE REASSURANCE

To offer false reassurance is to distance yourself from the person you are attempting to help. When someone has experienced the death of someone loved, false reassurance often leaves feelings of loneliness, misunderstanding, and emptiness. This person often speaks in cliches like, "Time heals all wounds," "Everything is going to be just fine," or "Hang in there."

These kinds of statements fail to provide the reassurance intended. Instead, the person whose feelings do not agree with such comments is convinced that you certainly do not understand.

This person seems to think they can make someone's grief just go away. But again, this pattern of communication is not respectful because it does not take into consideration the person's understanding of the way things are. You will be better off exploring painful realities than to communicate an attitude of false reassurance.

DISCOURAGING THE EXPRESSION
OF EMOTIONS AND TEARS

Unfortunately, many people associate tears of grief with personal inadequacy and weakness. Crying on the part of the mourner often generates feelings of helplessness in friends, family, and caregivers. Funeral directors are not immune from this tendency to feel helpless either.

Out of a wish to protect the mourner from pain, those people surrounding the mourner may serve to discourage the experience of tears. Comments similar to, "Tears won't bring him back," and "He wouldn't want you to cry" inhibit the expression of tears. Yet, crying is nature's way of releasing internal tension in the body and allowing the mourner to communicate a need to be comforted.

Becoming a helping funeral director means making a commitment to allowing people to share their pain with you. Obviously, you can not and should not try to discourage whatever emotions the person may be experiencing.

EMOTIONAL DISTANCING

Distancing can occur in helping relationships in different ways. Literal detachment occurs when you simply perform the required tasks while maintaining a sense of personal aloofness and distance. In this situation, the people with whom you interact will probably feel isolated and sense a lack of the characteristics of warmth and caring as outlined in Chapter 3.

Another form of detachment is to avoid discussion of painful issues. This is often done in an effort to protect the person you are helping and yourself from confronting the reality of the feelings. In actuality, healing comes from the expression of these painful feelings. By confronting the painful issues, you will experience deeper and more meaningful relationships with the people who have turned to you for help.

Make note of any additional destructive communication patterns of which you are aware. Then discuss these additional patterns with the group participants in this training.

ACTIVITY 15.1
GROUP REHEARSAL WITH TRAINER
OVERCOMING COMMUNICATION BARRIERS

Directions

The trainer will ask the group to provide examples they may have seen of any of the communication barriers outlined in this chapter.

Expectations

This will allow everyone to discuss any questions they have and serve to improve their overall communication skills.

After discussing each pattern the trainer will model the behavior to enable the participants to see, hear, and experience the effects. Participants will be encouraged to ask follow-up questions and clarify any misunderstandings related to the skill.

ACTIVITY 15.2
TRIAD BREAK-OUT REHEARSAL
OVERCOMING COMMUNICATION BARRIERS

Directions

Work in triads. One person (speaker) should talk freely to another person about any topic of interest. The second person (helper-listener, or, in this situation the communication stopper) will respond with a combination of the barriers to communication outlined in this chapter. The third person will be available to provide follow-up feedback on the process that occurs. Yes, probably some funny moments will occur and you are allowed to laugh occasionally!

Activity 15.2 (Continued)

Each member of the triad will rotate through each of the three roles: speaker, helper-listener, and observer. The trainer will circulate throughout the room and be available for questions and concerns.

Expectations

This will allow participants to work to overcome any of these barriers to effective interpersonal communication.

SUMMARY OUTCOMES OF CHAPTER

After reading and participating in the activities outlined in this chapter you should be able to (1) identify six barriers to effective communication; (2) discuss why these patterns are counterproductive in interpersonal relationships; and (3) eliminate any of these patterns from one's interpersonal way of being.

CHAPTER 16

THE INTEGRATION AND IMPLEMENTATION OF FUNERAL DIRECTOR HELPING SKILLS

"What we have to learn to do, we learn by doing."

Aristotle

ENHANCING SKILLS THROUGH PRACTICE

You have learned a number of essential helping skills in an effort to become a more effective funeral director. Your goal at this point is to integrate and implement these skills into everyday practice.

We have all heard about the importance of "PRACTICE, PRACTICE, PRACTICE." To know about interpersonal skills is one thing; to integrate them into your everyday "way of being" is another thing. That is why extensive use of activities and role-playing are essential to developing successfully the effective use of the skills outlined in this training.

This chapter focuses on providing a framework for extensive practice of your newly learned skills. At this point in the training, we will focus on extended role-playing allowing you to sharpen your newly learned skills. The activities that follow will provide a framework for enhancing your interpersonal skills with practice.

ACTIVITY 16.1
GROUP OBSERVATION OF TRAINER
INTEGRATION OF SKILLS

Directions

The trainer will provide an extended role-play (approximately 10 to 15 minutes) modeling the use of a wide variety of the skills outlined in this training. This will allow participants to observe the use of these skills in an integrated interaction.

A volunteer will be asked to role-play with the trainer. All remaining participants will use one of the "Observation Sheets" found in this chapter. Upon conclusion of the role-play a debriefing discussion will be held with the entire group.

Expectations

Participants will be encouraged to ask follow-up questions and clarify any misunderstandings related to any of the skills observed. Thus an integration of skills should become more meaningful to participants.

ACTIVITY 16.2
TRIAD BREAK-OUT REHEARSAL
INTEGRATION OF HELPING SKILLS

Directions

Work in triads. The purpose of this activity is to provide participants with the opportunity to practice the use of a variety of skills in an extended role-play (approximately 10 to 15 minutes).

Activity 16.2 (Continued)

One person (speaker) should serve as the person the funeral director (helper-listener) will assist. The helper-listener will practice the use of as many newly learned interpersonal skills as possible. You should not expect that every skill will necessarily be used. The third person will use one of the "Observation Sheets" found in this chapter. Upon conclusion of the role-play the triad members will discuss this experience using the information outlined by the observer.

Expectations

Strengths observed and areas that need continued work will be discussed in detail.

OBSERVATION SHEETS

Two observation sheets are provided in the remaining portion of this chapter. Observation Sheet I (Figure 16.1) will be completed by each person as he or she observes the trainer role-model these skills (see Activity 16.1). Observation Sheet II (Figure 16.2) can be completed by you when you are in the role of the observer in the break-out rehearsal (see Activity 16.2).

SUMMARY OUTCOMES OF CHAPTER

After reading and participating in the activities outlined in this chapter you should be able to (1) serve as a supportive observer of effective interpersonal skills, and (2) demonstrate the integrated use of the skills outlined in this text.

OBSERVATION SHEET I

Listed below are the skills covered throughout the training sessions. This outline will aid you in making observations when you are in the role of observer. The goal is to help the person you are observing become more aware of those skills he or she is using effectively and the ones that he or she may need to develop.

Person Observed: _____

Observer: _____ Date: _____

A. Brief Description of Role-playing Situation

_____

_____

_____

_____

_____

B. Observed Skills

Please circle the number of those skills used by the person you are observing. Rate the skill observed during the role-play by checking high, medium, or low for each skill observed.

	HIGH	MEDIUM	LOW
1. Characteristics of the Helping Funeral Director			
a. Empathy	____	____	____
b. Respect	____	____	____
c. Warmth and Caring	____	____	____
d. Genuineness	____	____	____
e. Self-disclosure	____	____	____

Figure 16.1. Observation Sheet I.

Figure 16.1. (Continued)

---

2. Attending

3. Paraphrasing

4. Clarifying

5. Perception Checking

6. Leading

7. Questioning

8. Reflecting Feelings

9. Informing

10. Summarizing

C. Barriers to Effective Communication

Circle the number of any of the following barriers to effective communication you have observed as outlined in Chapter 15.

1. Funeral Director Dominance

2. Bombarding with Questions

3. Inappropriate Self-disclosure

4. Offering Platitudes or False Reassurance

5. Discouraging the Expression of Emotions and Tears

6. Emotional Distancing

D. Comments/Observations of Behaviors

Please list. _____

_____

_____

_____

_____

_____

Figure 16.1. (Continued).

_____

E. Strengths Observed

Please list. _____

_____

_____

_____

_____

_____

_____

F. Suggested Areas on Which the Person Might Continue to Work

Please list. _____

_____

_____

_____

_____

_____

_____

G. General Comments and Observations

(Add suggestions for improvement.) _____

_____

_____

_____

_____

_____

_____

OBSERVATION SHEET II

Listed below are the skills covered throughout the training sessions. This outline will aid you in making observations when you are in the role of observer. The goal is to help the person you are observing become more aware of those skills he or she is using effectively and the ones that he or she may need to develop.

Person Observed: _____

Observer: _____ Date: _____

A. Brief Description of Role-playing Situation

_____

_____

_____

_____

_____

B. Observed Skills

Please circle the number of those skills used by the person you are observing. Rate the skill observed during the role-play by checking high, medium, or low for each skill observed.

	HIGH	MEDIUM	LOW
1. Characteristics of the Helping Funeral Director			
a. Empathy	____	____	____
b. Respect	____	____	____
c. Warmth and Caring	____	____	____
d. Genuineness	____	____	____
e. Self-disclosure	____	____	____

Figure 16.2. Observation Sheet II.

Figure 16.2. (Continued)

---

2. Attending   _____   _____   _____

3. Paraphrasing   _____   _____   _____

4. Clarifying   _____   _____   _____

5. Perception Checking   _____   _____   _____

6. Leading   _____   _____   _____

7. Questioning   _____   _____   _____

8. Reflecting Feelings   _____   _____   _____

9. Informing   _____   _____   _____

10. Summarizing   _____   _____   _____

C. Barriers to Effective Communication

Circle the number of any of the following barriers to effective communication you have observed as outlined in Chapter 15.

1. Funeral Director Dominance

2. Bombarding with Questions

3. Inappropriate Self-disclosure

4. Offering Platitudes or False Reassurance

5. Discouraging the Expression of Emotions and Tears

6. Emotional Distancing

D. Comments/Observations of Behaviors

Please list. _____

_____

_____

_____

_____

_____

_____

Figure 16.2. (Continued)

E. Strengths Observed

Please list. _____

_____

_____

_____

_____

_____

_____

F. Suggested Areas on Which the Person Might Continue to Work

Please list. _____

_____

_____

_____

_____

_____

_____

G. General Comments and Observations

(Add suggestions for improvement.) _____

_____

_____

_____

_____

_____

_____

PART IV

GRIEF
AND
MOURNING

CHAPTER **17**

UNDERSTANDING GRIEF AND MOURNING

"I thought I could describe a state; make a map of my sorrow. Sorrow, however, turns out to be not a state, but a process. It needs not a map but a history. There is a something new to be chronicled each and every day. Grief is like a long valley where any bone may reveal a totally new landscape."

C. S. Lewis

A major theme of this text is that the most important item you have to offer families you serve is yourself. As you make an effort to enhance your understanding of grief, you become capable of increasing your overall effectiveness as a caregiver.

No, you are not expected to be a professional "grief counselor." However, your vocational choice demands a working knowledge of the experience of grief. This chapter hopefully will be particularly helpful to those persons involved in providing structured post funeral service follow-up programs.

Learning about grief will enhance not only your own future, but the future of funeral service. The people you help before, during, and after the funeral will become walking-talking testimony to the value of funeral service. Working with people in acute grief requires the most sensitive and compassionate use of effective interpersonal skills. The purpose of this chapter is to introduce you briefly to the experience of grief and practical ways of helping the bereaved.

DISPELLING FIVE COMMON MYTHS ABOUT GRIEF

An appropriate place to begin is to identify, describe, and dispel five common myths about grief. Providing quality care to the bereaved requires that we as a society work to dispel these myths which are outlined in this section. People who have internalized these myths, including funeral service personnel, become incapable of helping grievers move toward healing.

These myths are not intended to be all-inclusive or mutually exclusive. Observation suggests that many people who believe in any one of these also will believe in many, if not all, of the others. Our joint task is not to condemn these people, but to encourage them supportively to broaden their understanding of the complex experiences of grief and mourning.

Myth #1: Grief and Mourning Are the Same Experience

The majority of people tend to use the words grief and mourning synonymously. However, an important distinction exists between them. We have learned that people move toward healing not by just grieving, but through mourning.

If we want to help the bereaved, we can work to understand the semantic distinctions of these commonly used terms. Simply stated, **grief** is the thoughts and feelings that are experienced within oneself upon the death of someone loved. In other words, grief is the internal meaning given to the experience of bereavement.

Mourning is taking the internal experience of grief and expressing it outside of oneself. The specific ways in which people express mourning are influenced by customs of their culture. Another way of defining mourning is to state that it is "grief gone public" or "sharing one's grief outside of oneself."

In reality, many people in our culture grieve, but they do not mourn. As opposed to being encouraged to express their grief outwardly they are often greeted with messages along the lines of "carry on," "keep your chin up," and "keep busy." So, they end up grieving within themselves in isolation, instead of mourning outside of themselves in the presence of loving companions.

Now that these terms have been defined in a more formal sense, let's take a moment to acknowledge that grief and mourning are much more personal experiences than their words describe. Actually, this author finds words inadequate to convey what grief and mourning are all about.

Grief and mourning are much more than words. Experiencing thoughts and feelings of grief is often movement through an unknown territory that is embraced by an overwhelming sense of pain and loss. Only through encouraging ourselves and others to mourn outside of ourselves will we become a catalyst for healing.

Don't just grieve, mourn, too, and be proud of your capacity to do so!

Myth #2: A Predictable and Orderly Stage-like Progression Exists to the Experience of Mourning

Stage-like thinking about both dying and mourning has been appealing to many people. Somehow the "stages of grief" have helped people try to make sense out of an experience that isn't as orderly and predictable as we would like it to be. Attempts have been made to replace fear and lack of understanding with the security that everyone grieves by going through the same stages. If only it were so simple!

The concept of "stages" was popularized in 1969 with the publication of Elizabeth Kubler-Ross' landmark text *On Death and Dying* (1969). Kubler-Ross never intended for people to interpret literally her five "stages of dying." However, many people have done just that and the consequences often have been disastrous.

One such consequence is when people around the grieving person adopt a rigid system of beliefs about grief that do not allow for the natural unfolding of the mourner's personal experience. We have come to understand that each person's grief is uniquely his or her own. As helpers we only get ourselves in trouble when we try to prescribe what someone's grief experience should be.

Just as people die in different ways, people mourn in different ways. Expecting anything less would be to demonstrate a lack of respect for the uniqueness of the person. This author prefers a helping attitude that conveys the following: "Teach me about your grief and I will be with you. As you teach me I will follow the lead you provide me and attempt to be a stabilizing and empathetic presence."

To think that one's goal as a caregiver is to move people through the stages of grief would be a misuse of counsel. A variety of unique thoughts and feelings will be experienced as part of the healing process. For example, disorganization, fear, guilt, and anger may or may not occur. Often, regression occurs along the way and invariably some overlapping. Sometimes emotions follow each other within a short period of time; at other times, two or more emotions are present in the grieving person simultaneously.

Do not prescribe how someone should grieve, but allow them to teach you where they are in the process.

Myth #3: The Best Procedure Is to Move Away from Grief Instead of Toward It

The unfortunate reality is that many grievers do not give themselves permission or receive permission from others to mourn, to express their many thoughts and feelings. We continue to live in a society that often encourages people prematurely to move away from their grief instead of toward it. The result is that many people either grieve in isolation or attempt to run away from their grief through various means (Wolfelt, 1987).

During ancient times, stoic philosophers encouraged their followers not to mourn, believing that self-control was the appropriate response to sorrow. Still today, well intentioned but uninformed people carry on this long-held tradition. A vital task of the helper is to encourage and support the movement toward an outward expression of grief.

One of the reasons for many people's preoccupation with the very question "how long does grief last?" often is related to society's impatience with grief and the desire to move people away from the experience of mourning. Shortly after the funeral (if a funeral is held) the grieving person is expected to "be back to normal."

Persons who continue to express their grief outwardly are often viewed as "weak," "crazy," or "self-pitying." The reality is that many people view grief as something to be overcome rather than experienced.

The result of these kinds of messages is to encourage the repression of the griever's thoughts and feelings. Refusing to allow tears, suffering in silence, and "being strong," are thought to be admirable behaviors. Many people in grief have internalized society's message that mourning should be done quietly, quickly, and efficiently.

Returning to the routine of work shortly after the death of someone loved, the bereaved person relates, "I'm fine," in essence saying "I'm not mourning." Friends, family, and coworkers often encourage this stance and refrain from talking about the death. The bereaved person, having an apparent absence of mourning (having moved away from their grief instead of toward it), tends to be more socially accepted by those around him or her.

However, this type of collaborative pretense surrounding grief does not meet the emotional needs of the bereaved person. Instead, the survivor is likely to feel further isolated in the experience of grief, with the eventual onset of the "going crazy syndrome." Attempting to mask or move away from the grief results in internal anxiety and confusion. With little, if any, social recognition related to the pain of the grief, the person often begins to think that his or her thoughts and feelings are abnormal. As a matter of fact, the most frequent initial comment of grieving persons at our Center for Loss and Life Transition in Colorado is the statement, "I think I'm going crazy."

Our society encourages people to move away prematurely from their grief instead of toward it. If we want to help bereaved people, we must remember that through the process of moving toward pain we move toward eventual healing.

**Myth #4: Following the Death
of Someone Significant to You,
the Goal Is to "Get Over" Your Grief**

We have all had the unfortunate experience of hearing people inquire of the bereaved person, "Are you over it yet?" Or, even worse yet, we hear people comment, "Well, they should be over it by now." To think that we as human beings "get over" our grief is ludicrous!

The final dimension of grief is a number of proposed models which is often referred to as resolution, recovery, reestablishment, or reorganization. This dimension often suggests a total return to "normalcy," and yet in my personal as well as professional experience, everyone is changed by the experience of grief.

For the mourner to assume that life will be exactly as it was prior to the death is unrealistic and potentially damaging. Recovery as understood by some persons, mourners and caregivers alike, all too often is seen erroneously as an absolute, a perfect state of reestablishment.

Reconciliation (Wolfelt, 1988) is a term this author believes to be more expressive of what occurs as the person works to integrate the new reality of moving forward in life without the physical presence of the person who has died. What occurs is a renewed sense of energy and confidence, an ability to fully acknowledge the reality of the death, and the capacity to become reinvolved with the activities of living. Also, an acknowledgement occurs that pain and grief are difficult yet necessary parts of life and living.

As the experience of reconciliation unfolds, the mourner recognizes that life will be different without the presence of the significant person who has died. A realization occurs that *reconciliation is a process, not an event.* Beyond an intellectual working through is an emotional working through.

What has been understood at the "head" level is now understood at the "heart" level—the person who was loved is dead.

The pain changes from being ever-present, sharp, and stinging to an acknowledged feeling of loss that has given rise to renewed meaning and purpose. The sense of loss does not completely disappear, yet softens, and the intense pangs of grief become less frequent. Hope for a continued life emerges as the griever is able to make commitments to the future, realizing that the dead person will never be forgotten, yet knowing that one's own life can and will move forward.

We never "get over" our grief but instead become reconciled to it. Those people who think the goal is to "resolve" grief become destructive to the healing process.

Myth #5: Tears Expressing Grief Are Only a Sign of Weakness

Unfortunately, many people associate tears of grief with personal inadequacy and weakness. Crying on the part of the mourner often generates feelings of helplessness in friends, family, and caregivers.

Out of a wish to protect the mourner from pain, those people surrounding the mourner may serve to inhibit the experience of tears. Comments similar to, "Tears won't bring him back" and "He wouldn't want you to cry" discourage the expression of tears. Yet crying is nature's way of releasing internal tension in the body and allows the mourner to communicate a need to be comforted.

Another function of crying is postulated in the context of attachment theory wherein tears are intended to bring about reunion with the lost person. While the reunion cannot occur, crying is thought to be biologically based and a normal way of attempting to reconnect with the person who has died. The frequency and intensity of crying eventually wanes as the hoped-for reunion does not occur.

While research in this area is still limited, some investigators have suggested that suppressing tears may increase susceptibility to stress-related disorders. This would seem to make sense in that crying is an exocrine process, one of the excretory processes. In reviewing other excretory processes, such as sweating and exhaling, the fact is that they all involve the removal of waste product from the body. Crying may serve a similar function.

In this author's clinical experience with thousands of people in grief, changes in physical expression have been observed following the expression of tears. While this is purely a subjective observation, seemingly not only do people feel better after crying, they also look better. Expressions of tension and agitation seem to flow out of their body. The capacity to express tears appears to allow for a genuine healing.

The expression of tears is not a sign of weakness. The capacity of the mourner to share tears is an indication of the willingness to do the "work of mourning."

SUMMARY RELATED TO MYTHS

Again, be aware that the above myths are not intended to be all-inclusive. This author suggests that the reader develop a list of any additional "grief myths" observed in our society.

Being surrounded by people who believe in these myths invariably results in a heightened sense of isolation and aloneness in the grieving person. The inability to be supported in the "work of mourning" destroys much of the capacity to enjoy life, living, and loving.

Only when we as a society are able to dispel these myths will grieving people experience the healing they deserve.

REFERENCES

Kubler-Ross, E. (1969). *On death and dying.* New York: Macmillan.

Lewis, C.S. (1961). *A grief observed.* Greenwich, CT: Seabury Press.

Wolfelt, A.D. (1987). Understanding common patterns of avoiding grief. *Thanatos,* Vol. 12:2, pp. 2-5.

Wolfelt, A.D. (1988). Resolution versus reconciliation: The importance of semantics. *Thanatos,* Vol. 12:4, pp. 10-13.

CHAPTER **18**

UNIQUENESS OF
GRIEF RESPONSE

We have already reminded ourselves that people mourn in different ways. To expect every family you serve to respond to a death in the same way would be inappropriate. Perhaps a helpful procedure at this point would be to review some of the many factors that influence how different people respond to the death of someone.

While ten factors are outlined in this section of this book, they are not intended to be all-inclusive. However, your awareness of these influences should prove to enhance your capacity to understand and assist bereaved families. Following each factor are guidelines in the form of questions for you as a helper to keep in mind as you enter the helping relationship. These questions should be of real importance to anyone involved in post-funeral service follow-up.

1. NATURE OF THE RELATIONSHIP
WITH THE PERSON WHO DIED

Different persons will have their own unique responses to the same loss based on the relationship that existed between self and the person that died. For example, with the death of a parent, observers will note that adult children will often grieve in totally different ways. This is only natural based on such influences as the prior attachment in the relationship and the function the relationship served for them. We know, for example, that relationships that have had strong components of ambivalence are more difficult to reconcile than those not as conflicted.

Questions to Ask Self as Helper

a. What was the nature of the relationship that existed between the grieving person and the person who died?

b. What was the nature of the level of attachment in the relationship?

c. What functions did the relationship serve in this person's life?

2. AVAILABILITY, HELPFULNESS, AND ABILITY OF THE PERSON TO MAKE USE OF A SOCIAL SUPPORT SYSTEM

The lack of a consistent, stabilizing support system typically results in a difficult, if not impossible, reconciliation process. To heal in one's grief requires an environment of empathy, support, and encouragement.

On occasion, you will observe a person who would appear to have a support system of family and friends, only to discover that little compassion or support is in the environment. When this is the situation, the person is lacking a vital ingredient that aids in the reconciliation. You also will witness those persons who have support available for a relatively short period of time after the death, only to have this support rapidly dwindle in weeks that follow. Again, for healing to occur, social support must be ongoing.

Some persons do not make effective use of a social support system that is, in fact, available to them. Those persons often isolate themselves and have difficulty accepting others' concern and support.

Questions to Ask Self as Helper

   a. Does the person have a positive support system available?

   b. Is this support available on an extended basis?

   c. Is the person able and willing to accept support from other persons?

3. UNIQUE CHARACTERISTICS OF THE BEREAVED PERSON

Previous styles of responding to loss and other crises often are, to some extent, predictive of a person's response to the death of a loved person. If a person has always tried to keep himself or herself distant or run away from crises, he or she may well follow this pattern when confronted with grief. However, if a person has always tended to confront crises head-on and express many thoughts and feelings, he or she will likely follow this pattern of behavior.

Other personality factors such as self-esteem, values, and beliefs also impact on the bereaved person's unique response to grief. Any prior mental health problems also might influence a person's response to loss.

Questions to Ask Self as Helper

   a. How has this person responded to prior loss or crises in his or her life?

   b. What was this person's personality like prior to the loss, particularly as it relates to self-esteem?

   c. Any previous history of mental health related difficulties, particularly as it relates to depression?

4. UNIQUE CHARACTERISTICS OF THE PERSON WHO DIED

Just as the characteristics of the bereaved person are reflected in the experience of grief, so, too, are the characteristics of the person who died. For example, some person's personality has been such that he or she has never been very easy to live with. With that person's death, survivors often experience ambivalent feelings. While they may miss the person, often other things about the person they do not miss. An illustration of this is when an alcoholic dies. The surviving family may miss the person; however, they are often relieved that they do not have to experience some of the person's behavior.

At the other end of the spectrum is the person whose personality was such that he or she was always a soothing, stabilizing influence within the family. The person managed to "keep the family together." In the absence of the stabilizing force, the surviving family often breaks down and can no longer function in the manner that it once did.

Questions to Ask Self as Helper

a. What was the personality of the person who died like?

b. Based on the person's unique personality, what role did he or she play within the family, i.e., stabilizer, disrupter, etc.?

5. THE NATURE OF THE DEATH

The circumstances surrounding the death have a tremendous impact on the survivor's grief. Included among the circumstances of which the helper should be aware are the age of the person who died, an anticipated death versus a sudden death, and any sense of having been able to have prevented the death.

The age of the person who died can have an impact on the psychological acceptance of the death. For example, within the order of the world we anticipate that parents will die before their children. When a child dies it is an assault of the natural course of events. The death of children in our culture is always seen as being untimely. Another example of the impact of age is the 40-year-old person who is thought to be in the "prime of life" who dies.

Numerous studies have addressed the reality that having the opportunity to anticipate a death assists in the griever's adaption to the loss. Sudden, unexpected loss, obviously does not allow the griever any opportunity for psychological preparation. Having the opportunity to anticipate a death does not lessen one's grief; however, it does provide time to prepare and attempt to understand the reality of the death.

Those persons that have persistent thoughts that they should have been able to have prevented the death typically experience more prolonged and severe grief reactions. While it is very natural for one to assess one's culpability upon the death of someone loved, some persons continue to blame themselves over a period of time. While a sense of preventability at times evolves from the griever's own unrealistic perceptions, you will see some persons whose behavior, in fact, could have impacted on the outcome of the death that occurred. One example of this is the person who fell asleep when driving an automobile, with an accident resulting in the death of a passenger.

Questions to Ask Self as Helper

a. What were the circumstances surrounding the death?

b. How old was the person who died?

c. What is the survivor's perception of the timeliness of the death?

d. Was the death anticipated or was it sudden and unexpected?

e. Does the person have a persistent sense that he or she should have been able to have prevented the death?

6. PERSON'S RELIGIOUS AND CULTURAL HISTORY

The grieving person's response to death is impacted by unique cultural and religious backgrounds. Different cultures are known for the various ways in which they express or repress their grief. The capacity to respect these differences enhances the helper's effectiveness. Individual differences secondary to religious and cultural backgrounds may assist or detract from the person's journey toward reconciliation of the loss.

Questions to Ask Self as Helper

a. What is the survivor's religious and cultural background?

b. How do these backgrounds influence the person's ability to give himself or herself permission to mourn?

c. What can this person teach me about his or her religious and cultural backgrounds?

7. OTHER CRISES OR STRESSES IN THE PERSON'S LIFE

An individual loss seldom occurs in isolation. The death of someone loved often means the loss of financial security, the loss of one's long-time friends and perhaps the loss of one's community. The helper should always assess other stresses and losses occurring in the survivor's life. Examples would include the person who may have some physical disability, strained family or friend relationship, or is unemployed. These additional stresses are known to impact negatively the experiences of one's grief.

Questions to Ask Self as Helper

a. What other stresses does this person have impacting on his or her life at this time?

b. What additional losses have resulted in his or her life from the death of this person?

8. PREVIOUS EXPERIENCES WITH DEATH

We now live in what has been termed by the sociologist Robert Fulton as "the world's first death-free generation." This means that it is now possible for a person to grow into adulthood without having experienced a close personal loss. For these persons who have had no previous experience with death, no opportunity has been present to develop resources to cope. In addition, prior negative associations with death can influence one's capacity to grieve in a healthy way. For example, if someone has learned to avoid death and run away from its reality, chances are this pattern will be adopted in the future.

Questions to Ask Self as Helper

    a.   What is the survivor's previous experience with death?

    b.   How have these previous experiences influenced the person's attitudes and behaviors related to grief?

9. SOCIAL EXPECTATIONS BASED ON THE SEX OF THE SURVIVOR

This relates to how males and females are taught differently about expressing their feelings. Generally men are encouraged to "be strong" and restrain themselves from the expression of painful emotions. Typically, men have more difficulty in allowing themselves to be helpless than women do. Women often experience difficulty in expressing feelings of anger, whereas men tend to be more quick to express explosive emotions. The key here is to respect the ways the person has been socialized, based on sex, to respond in the face of loss in his or her life. The task of the helper is not to change their response, but to understand it and facilitate its healthy expression.

Question to Ask Self as Helper

How has this person been socially influenced to respond to loss based on his or her sex?

10. RITUAL OR FUNERAL EXPERIENCE

Decisions survivors make related to the experience of the funeral can either help or hinder the journey through grief. In spite of frequent criticism, funerals assist in social, psychological, and spiritual reconciliation after a death. Numerous research findings have confirmed the value of the funeral. Many people who experience complicated grief, relate that their experience with the funeral was minimized or inadequate in some way.

The funeral can serve as a time to honor the person who has died, bring survivors close together for needed support, affirm that life goes on, and give mourners a context of meaning related to their own religious or philosophical backgrounds. If the purpose of the funeral is minimized or distorted in some way, the experience of reconciling one's grief often becomes more difficult.

Questions to Ask Self as Helper

a. What was this person's experience with the funeral?

b. Did the funeral experience aid in the expression or repression of the individual's grief?

c. What role does this person believe the funeral played in his or her experience with grief?

SUMMARY RELATED TO GRIEF RESPONSE

Again, keeping the above factors in mind will aid you in understanding the person's unique experience with grief. On occasion, you may find it helpful to review these influences, as well as those questions to ask yourself as a helper. Anyone doing follow-up should continually reassess these questions as you accompany the person in the "work of mourning."

CHAPTER 19

OVERVIEW OF NORMAL EXPERIENCE OF GRIEF

A vital task of funeral service personnel is to become familiar with those thoughts, feelings, and behaviors that may be expressed by the bereaved person. What follows is an overview of the normal adult grief process.

A number of observers have defined models of grief that are often referred to as "stages," e.g., Bowlby (1973), Engel (1971), Kubler-Ross (1969), Lindemann (1944), and Parkes (1972). Erich Lindemann's 1944 article on the "Symptomatology and Management of Acute Grief" was one of the first writings in this area. His observations were based on interviews with over 100 grieving persons who had experienced the death of family members in Boston's Coconut Grove restaurant fire. Lindemann and other authors most typically describe stages as moving from disorganization to reorganization or as moving from shock to recovery.

Our goal for the purposes of this chapter is to present a multidimensional model of an adult's grief experience. This model is based upon my personal experiences with loss, clinical experiences with grieving persons, and teachings from the literature. By no means do I pretend that this model is all-inclusive; however, I do hope it aids funeral service personnel in the understanding of the grief experience.

Not every person will experience each and every response described and certainly not necessarily in the order outlined. Some regression will occur along the way and invariably some overlapping. Unfortunately, as previously written, a person's response to loss is never as uncomplicated as described by the written word. You will note that the word "dimension" of grief, as opposed to "stage" of grief, is used in an effort to prevent thinking that the experience of grief occurs in some kind of ordered fashion.

Now, keeping in mind the uniqueness of each person's experience with grief, let's familiarize ourselves with some of the more common dimensions of the experience.

SHOCK/DENIAL/NUMBNESS/DISBELIEF

The constellation of experiences of shock, denial, numbness and disbelief is often nature's way of temporarily protecting the mourner from the reality of the death of someone loved. In reflecting on this experience, most mourners make comments like, "I was there, but yet I really wasn't," "It was like a dream," "I managed to do what needed to be done, but I didn't feel a part of it." Reports of feeling dazed and stunned are very common during this time.

When little, if any, opportunity occurs to anticipate a death, this constellation of experiences is typically heightened and prolonged. However, even when the death of someone loved is expected, we often see components of shock, denial, numbness and disbelief. This experience creates an insulation from the reality of the death until one is more able to tolerate what one doesn't want to believe. It serves as a "temporary time-out" or "psychological shock absorber." Our emotions need time to catch up with what our minds have been told. At one level, the mourner knows the person is dead, yet is not able or willing to believe it.

This constellation of experiences acts as an anesthetic; the pain is there, but you do not experience it in its full reality. In a very real sense the body and mind take over in an effort to help the person survive. Typically a physiological component to this experience includes a takeover by the autonomic nervous system. Heart palpitations, queasiness, stomach pain, and dizziness are among the most common experiences.

A wide spectrum of what might be termed bizarre behaviors in other contexts is often observed. Hysterical crying, outbursts of anger, laughing, and fainting are frequently witnessed at this time. In actuality, expressing these behaviors allows for survival. Unfortunately, people around mourners at this time will often try to suppress these experiences.

This dimension of the grief experience typically reflects only the beginning of the person's journey through grief. However, important to note is that many people, both lay and professionals, acknowledge these manifestations as the entire mourning process. This phenomenon is reflected in the often heard comment from the bereaved person: "People were there for me right at the time of the death and for a short time thereafter, but they quickly returned to their routines and seemed to forget about me and my need for support and understanding." These kinds of statements tell helpers something very important about not only being available at the time of the death, but for a long time thereafter. This also helps explain the increasing interest in post funeral service follow-up programs.

The process of beginning to embrace the full reality of the death and move beyond this dimension of one's grief varies widely. Shock and numbness wane only at the pace one is able and ready to acknowledge feelings of loss. To provide a specific time frame for everyone would be to overgeneralize. However, based on my personal experiences, clinical experiences, and knowledge of the literature, commonly this spectrum of experiences is most intense during the first four- to six-week period immediately following the death of someone loved.

However, even after one becomes capable of embracing the reality of the loss, times still exist when this dimension comes to the surface. This is particularly seen at such times as the anniversary of death or other special occasions (birthdays, holidays, etc.). I also have repeatedly witnessed the resurgence of this dimension when the person visits a place associated with a special memory of the dead person.

In actuality, the person's mind approaches and retreats from the reality of a death over and over again, as he or she tries to embrace and integrate the meaning of the death into his or her life. The availability of a consistent support system allows this process to occur. During this process of acknowledging one's grief, the hope, at times, is that one will wake up from a bad dream and that none of this really happened.

DISORGANIZATION/CONFUSION/ SEARCHING/YEARNING

Often, the most isolating and frightening part of the experience of grief begins after the funeral. This is frequently when the mourner begins to be confronted with the reality of the death. As one woman expressed, "I felt as if I was a lonely traveler with no companion, and worse yet, no destination. It was as if I couldn't find myself or anybody else."

This is when many people experience the "going crazy syndrome." Because normal thoughts and behaviors in grief are so different from what one normally experiences, the grieving person does not know whether the behavior is normal or abnormal. The experiences described below are so common after the death of someone loved that they must be acknowledged as part of the normal process of mourning. A major task of the helper is to assist in normalizing these experiences.

Often present is a sense of restlessness, agitation, impatience, and ongoing confusion. An analogy that seems to fit is that it is like being in the middle of a wild, rushing river, whereby you can't get a grasp on anything. Disconnected thoughts race through the mourner's mind and strong emotions at times are overwhelming. Disorganization and confusion often manifest themselves in terms of an inability to complete any tasks. A project may get started but go unfinished. Time is distorted and seen as something to be endured. Certain times of day, often early morning and late night, are times when the person feels most disoriented and confused. Disorganization and confusion are often accompanied by fatigue and lack of initiative. The acute pain of the loss is devastating to the point that normal pleasures do not seem to matter.

A restless searching for the person who dies is a common part of the experience. Parkes (1972), Bowlby (1973), and others have written extensively about searching behavior. Yearning for the dead person and being preoccupied with memories of the individual have led to intense moments of distress. Often a shift in perception makes other people look like the dead person. A phenomenon sometimes occurs whereby sounds are interpreted as signals that the person has returned. For example, hearing the garage door open and the person entering the house as they had done for so many years.

Visual hallucinations occur so frequently that they cannot be considered abnormal. I personally prefer the term "memory picture" to visual hallucination. It seems that as part of the searching and yearning process the mourner not only experiences a sense of the dead person's presence, but may have transient experiences of looking across the room and seeing the person.

Other common features during this time are difficulties with eating and sleeping. Many people experience loss of appetite while others overeat. Those people who do eat often note a lack of being able to taste their food. Difficulty in going to sleep and early morning awakening also are common experiences.

Dreams about the dead person are often a part of the experience at this time. Dreams are often an unconscious means of searching for the person who has died. People often described to me that their dreams are an opportunity to be close to the person. As one widower related, "I find myself dreaming about my wife. I see us together, happy and content. If it only could be that way again." The content of these dreams often reflects the real life changes in the person's experience with mourning.

GENERALIZED
ANXIETY/PANIC/FEAR

Feelings of anxiety, panic, and fear are often experienced by the mourner. These feelings are typically generated from thoughts such as "Will my life have any purpose without this person? I don't think I can live without him." The death of someone loved naturally threatens one's feelings of security and results in the evolution of anxiety.

As the person's mind is continually brought back to the pain of the loss, panic may set in. Anxiety and fear often relate to thoughts about "going crazy." The thought of being abnormal creates even more intense fear.

Fear of what the future holds, fear that if one person dies, will another?, increased awareness of one's own mortality, feelings of vulnerability about being able to survive without the person, inability to concentrate, and emotional and physical fatigue all serve to heighten anxiety, panic, and fear. The mourner often feels overwhelmed by everyday problems and concerns. To make matters worse, a change may occur in economic status, large bills to be paid, and the fear of becoming dependent on others.

PHYSIOLOGICAL CHANGES

A person's body responds to what the mind has been told at a time of acute grief. Some of the most common physiological changes that the mourner may experience are as follows:

> generalized lack of energy and fatigue,
> shortness of breath,
> feelings of emptiness in the stomach,
> tightness in the throat and chest,
> sensitivity to noise,
> heart palpitations,
> queasiness,
> difficulty in sleeping or
>   on other occasions prolonged sleeping,
> headaches, and
> agitation and generalized tension.

With loss, the mourner's immune system breaks down and he or she becomes more vulnerable to illness. Many studies have documented significant increases in illness following bereavement.

In the majority of instances, physical symptoms are normal and temporary. At times, the mourner will unconsciously assume a "sick role" in an effort to legitimize his or her feelings to others. This often results in frequent visits to the physician. Unfortunately, assumption of the "sick role" often occurs when the person does not receive encouragement to mourn, or doesn't give self permission to express thoughts and feelings in other ways.

EXPLOSIVE EMOTIONS

Because of society's attitude toward anger, this dimension is often the most upsetting to those persons around the griever. Often, both the mourner and those persons trying to be supportive to the mourner have problems acknowledging and creating an environment for the expression of this wide spectrum of emotions. The reason for this is frequently related to the uncertainty of how to respond to the griever at this time.

We sometimes oversimplify these emotions by talking only about anger. The mourner also may experience feelings of hate, blame, terror, resentment, rage, and jealousy. While these emotions all have their distinctive features, adequate similarities exist in the person's underlying needs to warrant discussing the various explosive emotions together. Beneath the explosive emotions are the griever's more primary feelings of pain, helplessness, frustration, fear, and hurt.

Expression of explosive emotions often relates to a desire to restore things to the way they were before the death. Even though a conscious awareness exists that the person has died, the need to express explosive emotions and a desire to "get the person back" seems to be grounded in psychobiological roots. As John Bowlby (1961) has observed:

> There are therefore good biological reasons for every separation to be responded to in an automatic instinctive way with aggressive behavior; irretrievable loss is statistically so unusual that it is not taken into account. In the course of our evolution, it appears our instinctual equipment has come to be so fashioned that all losses are assumed to be retrievable and are responded to accordingly.

So while the expression of explosive emotions does not create the desired result of bringing the dead back to life, we can hopefully understand the naturalness of its existence. If viewed in this fashion, anger and other related emotions can be seen as intelligent responses that the grieving person is making to restore the relationship that has been lost. Actually, in my experience, a healthy survival value exists in being able to temporarily protest the painful reality of the loss. It's as if having the capacity to express anger gives one the courage to survive at this particular point in time. The griever who either does not give self permission, or doesn't receive permission from others to protest, may slide into a chronic depressive response that includes no desire to go on living.

The fact that the dead person does not come back despite the griever's explosive emotions is part of the reality testing needed for the eventual process of reconciliation. With the gradual awareness that the person who has died will, in fact, not return, the need for the expression of these emotions changes over time.

Only when the reality that the loss is permanent creeps in does the person free himself or herself from this task of grieving. Should the explosive emotions become chronic, not changing over time, this would be an indication of a complicated grief response.

Outward Explosive Emotions

Explosive emotions basically have two avenues for expression: outward or inward. What the griever does with these emotions can have a powerful impact on the person's journey through grief. The anger may be expressed outwardly toward friends and family, the physician, God, the person who died, the funeral service personnel, people who have not experienced loss, or any number of other persons or places.

For our present purposes, let's briefly expand on anger that gets directed toward God. Some mourners perceive death to be a form of punishment and naturally respond with anger toward those they feel are responsible for the death. God, seen as having power over life and death, becomes a target for the expression of explosive emotions. For example, a protestant man remarked:

"I stopped attending church after my wife's death. She and I had been so devoted in our faith and yet He took her from me. I don't see any point in being faithful to Him if He is not going to be faithful to me."

As previously mentioned, another frequent target for the expression of anger is family members. In a study of the first year of bereavement, Glick, Weiss, and Parkes (1974) noted that widows were angry at family members for lack of support, for overprotection, and for disappointment in expected help from relatives. Among other things, anger also was reported over funeral details, withdrawal, and at the eagerness of relatives to acquire possessions of the person who died.

Inward Explosive Emotions

In some instances, mourners will direct their anger inward resulting in low self-esteem, depression, chronic feelings of guilt, physical complaints, and potentially suicide. When anger is repressed and directed inward, the person's experience with grief often becomes complicated and chronic. Anger turned inward may result in agitation, tension, and general restlessness. It is as if something is inside the person trying to get out.

Should you observe cues that lead you to believe that the mourner has turned his or her anger inward, it would be appropriate to refer the person to someone more experienced in counseling the bereaved.

GUILT/REMORSE/ ASSESSING CULPABILITY

We now recognize that guilt and self-blame are often seen in the grieving person. A natural process seems to occur of assessing one's culpability following loss through death. Some people become obsessed by guilt, leading to a complicated grief response and the need for specialized help, while others come to understand the normalcy of temporary feelings of guilt.

Guilt evolves in a number of ways as a part of the experience of grief. Perhaps the most common is the "If only I would have . . ." or "Why didn't I . . ." syndrome. This often relates to a sense of wanting to change the circumstances surrounding the death or unfinished business in the relationship with the person who died.

Some examples of common "if onlys" that you may hear the person express are as follows:

> If only I would have known he was dying.
> If only I would have gotten her to the doctor sooner.
> If only I had insisted that she take better care of herself.
> If only I had been a better wife.

These are only a few of hundreds of examples that could be given. While the expression of guilt is often not logical or real, it is still a natural part of the healing process. Unfortunately, as helpers, we often find ourselves wanting to rush in and try to take away the person's need to express guilt or self-blame.

Feelings of guilt are often expressed about the days or weeks just prior to the death of the person. Assessing one's culpability during this time often seems to be an indirect means of assuring oneself that they did everything they could have done for the person. This is most certainly an understandable need on the part of the survivor. A common theme I often witness at this time is a desire to have created opportunities to talk with the person about their dying. For example, "If only we could have been honest with each other about what was happening."

Surviving a person who has died often generates feelings of guilt. **Survival guilt** leads the person to ask, "How is it that they died and I survived?" I recently saw a middle-aged man in counseling who had been driving an automobile in which his wife was a passenger. He fell asleep at the wheel and there was an accident. His wife died instantly and he walked away without a scratch. He needed to be able to explore the question of his survival in the face of her death. In his mind, his sense of responsibility for falling asleep demanded his death, but certainly not his wife's.

Another type of guilt evolves when a person's death brings some sense of relief or release. This often occurs when the person who died had been ill for a prolonged period of time or the relationship was conflicted. In the case of a long illness, the mourner may not miss the frequent trips to the hospital or the physical responsibilities of caring for the person. If the person is not able to acknowledge this sense of relief as natural, and not equal to a lack of love, they may feel guilty for feeling relieved.

An example of the **relief-guilt** syndrome in a conflicted relationship is as follows: I have worked with a number of families who have experienced the death of an alcoholic member of their family. Upon the person's death, naturally certain behaviors the family does not miss. Again, if the survivors are able to be understanding of their sense of relief, all is well and good. However, they often get caught in the trap of the relief-guilt syndrome.

Another form of guilt is that which evolves from **long-standing personality factors** of the survivor. Some people are taught early in life, typically during childhood, that they are responsible when anything bad or unfortunate occurs. When a death occurs in their lives, the first place they look to find blame is at themselves. Obviously, this kind of guilt relates to long-standing personality factors that would have to be something to work on in the context of a professional counseling relationship.

Guilt also can be experienced when the mourner begins to re-experience any kind of joy or happiness in their life. This is often related to loyalty to the deceased and fears that being happy in some way betrays the relationship that once was. Opportunities to explore these feelings are often necessary as the person moves forward in the experience of the grief.

Survivors often witness feelings of guilt when they were not able to be present when the death occurred. Often the irrational, yet understandable thought is that, "If I had been there, the person would not have died." This often relates to a desire to have power or control over something which one has no power or control over. After all, if I feel guilty, it means I could have done something to change the outcome of what happened. The survivors, thinking that if they were present the outcome would have been different, seem to be attempting to counter a felt sense of helplessness and unimportance. Again, certainly an understandable response in the context of the painful reality of the loss.

You also will witness occasions when feelings of guilt will be induced by those persons around the griever. This often occurs through ignorance, lack of understanding, or the need to **project outside of oneself** onto others.

Projecting outside of oneself is illustrated by family members who, in wanting to deny their own pain and any sense of culpability, strike-out against other family members.

An unfortunate example of guilt induction is the family friend who informs the recently bereaved widow: "Your husband would not have died if you had had a closer relationship with God." These kinds of messages often become very destructive to the mourner who is already struggling with grief.

People sometimes feel guilty for having had a conscious or unconscious **wish for the death** toward the person who has died. This relates to the concept of magical thinking that somehow one's thoughts can cause action. The majority of relationships have components of ambivalence whereby a person will think on occasion, "I wish you would go away and leave me alone." Or, in highly conflicted relationships even more direct thoughts of wanting the relationship to end will have occurred. When the person does die, the survivor has a sense that they somehow caused the death.

While all relationships have periods of time when negative thoughts are experienced, obviously, one's mind does not have the power to inflict death on someone. Again, however, you can easily see how the person might connect his or her thoughts with events that occur.

Feelings of guilt are not limited to any select group of people. They are a natural part of the experience of grief. Being aware of the normalcy of guilt and the need to assess culpability hopefully allows you to enter the helping relationship with an open mind and an available presence.

LOSS/EMPTINESS/SADNESS

With good reason, this constellation of feelings and experiences is often the most difficult for the griever. The full sense of loss never occurs all at once. Often weeks, more often months, pass after the death before the person is confronted by how much his or her life is changed by the loss. A person that has been a vital part of one's life is no longer present. The mourner certainly has the right to have feelings of loss, emptiness, and sadness. Unfortunately, many people surrounding the mourner frequently try to take these feelings away from the person. Friends, family, and sometimes even professional caregivers erroneously believe that their job is to distract the mourner from these feelings.

At times the grieving person has intense feelings of loss and loneliness. When these experiences initially occur they are usually very frightening to the person. Thinking and hoping that he or she has already experienced the most devastating of these emotions, the person usually is unprepared for the depth of this experience.

Given the opportunity, the majority of mourners will share that the following times are among the most difficult: weekends; holidays; upon initially waking in the morning; late at night, particularly at bedtime; family meal times; upon arriving home to an empty house; and any kind of anniversary occasion. These difficult times usually have some special connection to the person who has died.

Loss, emptiness, and sadness may be intense enough to be considered **depression.** The literature contains much debate on grief concerning the distinction between grief and depression. Grief is accompanied by many symptoms of depression such as sleep disturbance, appetite disturbance, decreased energy, withdrawal, guilt dependency, lack of concentration, and a sense of losing control. Changes in one's normal capacity to function along with these and other depressive symptoms often result in the griever feeling isolated, helpless, and childlike. This normal repression that accompanies grief naturally impacts on one's sense of self-esteem and well-being. The person often needs help understanding that these characteristics of mourning are temporary and will change over time.

An important procedure is to note some differences between the normal depressive experience of grief and **clinical depression.** Recognizing that other caregivers may use other criteria, the following are some of the distinctions I find helpful to distinguish between depressive grief and other forms of depression.

In normal grief, the person responds to comfort and support; whereas, depressives often do not accept support.

The bereaved are often openly angry; whereas, the depressive complains and is irritable but does not directly express anger.

Bereaved persons can relate their depressed features to the loss they have experienced; whereas, depressives often do not relate their experience to any life event.

In normal grief, people can still experience moments of enjoyment in life; whereas, with the depressive an all pervading sense of doom seems to exist.

Those people around the griever can sense feelings of sadness and emptiness; whereas, depressives project a sense of hopelessness and chronic emptiness.

The griever is more likely to have transient physical complaints; whereas, the depressive has chronic physical complaints.

The griever often expresses guilt over some specific aspect of the loss; whereas, the depressive often has generalized feelings of guilt.

While the self-esteem of the griever is temporarily impacted upon, it is not the depth of loss of esteem usually observed in the depressive.

Obviously, to distinguish between the depression of grief and clinical forms of depressive illness is not always easy. If you should find yourself in doubt regarding a differential diagnosis between the two, the wise procedure is to consider consultation from other trained professionals. On some occasions loss precipitates a major depressive illness that may require specialized medical intervention, i.e., antidepressant medication.

Related to depressive features we should note that many mourners do have transient thoughts of suicide. Often the hope is of being reunited with the person who has died or that this will allow the survivor to escape the pain of the grief. While transient suicidal thoughts are normal and common, suicidal thoughts always should be assessed with utmost care. When in doubt, be certain to obtain the help and guidance of a professional counselor who is trained in the assessment of suicide risk.

Feelings of deprivation and impoverishment also are common during mourning. The person might long to be held, comforted, and simply wish to have that person who has died to talk to. Often the thought is, "The one person who understood me is gone and I feel abandoned." Well-known author C.S. Lewis (1961) expressed his sense of deprivation following the death of his wife when he wrote: "Thought after thought, feeling after feeling, action after action had Helen for their target. Now their target is gone. I keep on, through habit, fitting an arrow to the string, then I remember that I have to lay the bow down."

The person who is not in an environment conducive to acknowledging and exploring experiences of intense loss, emptiness, and sadness will sometimes be in the position of being in conflict about expressing these feelings. Suppressed feelings often push for release, while the person is either discouraged by others, by self, or by both to repress them. The frequent result is an increased sense of isolation, loss, and sadness.

RELIEF/RELEASE

Death can bring relief and release from suffering, particularly when the illness has been long and debilitating. Many people inhibit this normal dimension of their grief, fearing that others will think they are wrong or cruel to feel this way. So, while very natural, feelings of relief and release are often difficult for the griever to talk about and admit openly.

Relief does not equal a lack of feeling for the person who died, but instead relates to the griever's response to an end to painful suffering. In addition, to feel relief is natural because death frees one of certain demands and opens up new opportunities and experiences.

I recently saw a 40-year-old man in counseling following the death of his 38-year-old wife. His wife had been suffering with bone cancer for the past two years. Upon her death, he was able to acknowledge his relief that she was finally free of her pain. However, he also was able, with time, to acknowledge that the marital relationship of 16 years always had been conflicted and unsatisfactory to him. He expressed release from their constant fights and his perception of their mutual chronic unhappiness in the relationship.

Feelings of relief and release also relate to the reality that we do not just begin to grieve at the moment of someone's death. The experience of grief begins when the person with whom we have a relationship enters the transition from being alive and living to dying.

When the dying process is prolonged and filled with physical and emotional pain for those involved, one might observe that family members experience some of the following thoughts over time: Initially a sense of "he is sick," toward "he is very sick," toward "he may die," toward "he is going to die," toward "he is suffering too much," toward "I'll be glad when he is out of his pain," toward "he is dead," toward among a number of other thoughts and feelings "I'm relieved that he is dead and out of his pain."

This process of changing thought patterns and experiences over time relates to the concept of **anticipatory grief,** a term first used by Erich Lindemann (1944). Anticipatory grief is when emotional responses occur before an expected loss. To explore this concept in-depth would be to go beyond the primary purpose of this chapter. However, the reader is urged to familiarize himself or herself with this concept in the grief literature.

Death also can be experienced as relief when the apparent alternative is a continual debilitating journey with an unconscious vegetative form of existence, chronic alcoholism, and other forms of living that involve lack of quality. Regardless of how loving and caring a family may be, at times chronic illness exhausts and drains everyone. When death finally comes, relief is experienced not in isolation, but amongst a number of other emotions as well.

Another aspect of relief for some people is a sense of having been spared because someone else, not themselves, died. Again, this sense of relief is natural and some persons will express a need to explore these feelings with you.

Crying and expressing the thoughts and feelings related to a loss also can be experienced as relief. I often witness a tremendous sense of relief from persons who have repressed and avoided the outward expression of their grief. Being able to acknowledge the pain of their experience frequently relieves internal pressure and allows them to make movement in the journey through their grief. To the mourner a sense of relief can occur by finding someone who is able to communicate an empathetic understanding of one's experience.

The relief that comes from acknowledging the pain of grief becomes a critical step toward reconciliation. As the pain is explored, acknowledged, and accepted as a vital part of healing, a renewed sense of meaning and purpose follows. Working to embrace relief as one of many normal feelings creates the opportunity to find hope beyond one's acute grief.

RECONCILIATION

The final dimension of grief in a number of proposed models is often referred to as resolution, recovery, reestablishment, or reorganization. This dimension often suggests a total return to "normalcy," and yet in my personal, as well as professional experience, everyone is changed by the experience of grief. For the mourner to assume that life will be exactly as it was prior to the death is unrealistic and potentially damaging. Recovery as understood by some persons, mourners and caregivers alike, is all too often seen erroneously as an absolute, a perfect state of reestablishment.

Reconciliation is a term I believe to be more expressive of what occurs as the person works to integrate the new reality of moving forward in life without the physical presence of the person who has died. While we outlined this concept under our discussion of myths, it is so vital to understand that we will review it again here.

What occurs is a renewed sense of energy and confidence, an ability to fully acknowledge the reality of the death, and the capacity to become reinvolved with the activities of living. Also an acknowledgement occurs that pain and grief are difficult, yet necessary parts of life and living.

As the experience of reconciliation unfolds, the mourner recognizes that life will be different without the presence of the significant person who has died. A realization occurs that reconciliation is a process, not an event. Tasks involved in working through the completion of the emotional relationship with the person who has died, and redirecting of energy and initiative toward the future often take longer and involve more labor than most people are aware. We, as human beings, never "get over" our grief, but instead become reconciled to it.

We have noted that **the course of mourning cannot be prescribed** because it depends on many factors such as the nature of the relationship with the person who died, the availability and helpfulness of a support system, the nature of the death, and the ritual or funeral experience. As a result, despite how much we now know about dimensions of the grief experience, they will take different forms with different people. One of the major factors influencing the mourner's movement toward reconciliation is that he or she will be allowed to mourn in his or her own unique way and time.

Reconciliation is the dimension wherein the full reality of the death becomes a part of the mourner. Beyond an intellectual working through is an emotional working through. What has been understood at the "head" level is now understood at the "heart" level—the person who was loved is dead. When a reminder such as holidays, anniversaries, or other special memories are triggered, the mourner experiences the intense pain inherent in grief, yet the duration and intensity of the pain is typically less severe as the healing of reconciliation occurs.

The pain changes from being ever-present, sharp, and stinging to an acknowledged feeling of loss that has given rise to renewed meaning and purpose. The sense of loss does not completely disappear, yet softens, and the intense pangs of grief become less frequent. Hope for a continued life emerges as the griever is able to make commitments to the future, realizing that the dead person will never be forgotten, yet knowing that one's own life can and will move forward.

For more extensive information on the reconciliation process, the reader is referred to the article titled "Resolution versus Reconciliation: The Importance of Semantics" (Wolfelt, 1988).

ACTIVITY 19.1
REFLECTIONS ON DEATH EXPERIENCES

Directions

Form small groups of three to five people. Discuss some of the thoughts and feelings that result from completing the following five lead-ins:

1. My first experience with death was . . .

   _____

2. What I remember feeling about that death was . . .

   _____

3. The people around me responded to me by . . .

   _____

4. When I'm with someone experiencing the pain of grief, I feel . . .

   _____

5. When I die, I hope people will remember me in the following way . . .

   _____

REFERENCES

Bowlby, H. (1961). Processes of mourning. *International Journal of Psychoanalysis, 42,* pp. 317-340.

Bowlby, J. (1973). *Attachment and loss: Separation.* New York: Basic Books.

Engel, G.L. (1971). Sudden and rapid death during psychological stress. *Annals of Internal Medicine, 74,* pp. 771-782.

Glick, I.O. , Weiss, R.S., & Parkes, C.M. (1974). *The first year of bereavement.* New York: Wiley.

Kubler-Ross, E. (1969). *On death and dying.* New York: Macmillan.

Lewis, C.S. (1961). *A grief observed.* Geensich, CT: Seabury Press.

Lindemann, E. (1944). Symptomatology and management of acute grief. *American Journal of Psychiatry, 101, pp. 141-148.*

Parkes, C.M. (1972). *Bereavement: Studies of grief in life.* New York: International Universities Press.

Wolfelt, A.D. (1988). Resolution versus reconciliation: The importance of semantics. *Thanatos,* Vol. 12:4, pp. 10-13.

CHAPTER **20**

UNDERSTANDING COMMON PATTERNS OF AVOIDING GRIEF

Grief has been described as the emotions that heal themselves. While this may have been true at some point in history, we now realize that the majority of people need some social context for healing to occur. Grievers need the opportunity to share their grief outside of themselves in a caring environment.

The unfortunate reality is that many grievers do not give themselves permission, or receive permission from others, to mourn or to express their many conflicting thoughts and feelings. We live in a society that often encourages the repression of the emotions of grief, as opposed to the expression. The result is that many people either grieve in isolation or attempt to run away from their grief through various means.

During ancient times, stoic philosophers encouraged their followers not to grieve, believing that self-control was the appropriate response to sorrow. Still today, well-intentioned, but uninformed people carry on this long held tradition. Yet, we know that a major task of mourning is to acknowledge and express the full range of thoughts and feelings connected to the loss.

A vital role of those persons who desire to help the bereaved is to encourage and support the outward expression of grief. The grieving person moves toward reconciling self to the loss when he or she can attend to his or her emotional experiences, accepting them as a result of the privilege of having been capable of loving another person. A renewed sense of well-being has the opportunity to evolve, as caring people accept the griever for who he or she is, as he or she is, and where he or she is.

This chapter will

1. identify common patterns that bereaved people tend to adopt in their efforts to avoid the pain of grief,

2. define those avoidance patterns,

3. outline the consequences of adopting those avoidance patterns, and

4. reinforce the importance of encouraging the healthy expression of grief.

Again, persons working in post-funeral service follow-up should be aware of these patterns which are described on the pages that follow.

COMMON AVOIDANCE PATTERNS

While a number of unique ways exist by which persons repress or "move away" from the expression of their grief, we can work to identify common patterns that are adopted. The various patterns of avoiding grief are not mutually exclusive. Some people will experience a combination of patterns while others will maintain one primary mode of avoidance. The specific combination of patterns (or primary mode used most often) will depend on one's personal history, societal influences, and basic personality.

The destructive effect of the adopted pattern is typically directly proportional to the degree of avoidance. However, prolonged avoidance, whatever the degree, will always be destructive. In moving away from our feelings of grief, (that is, in repressing, denying, or deadening our feelings), we ultimately become destructive to ourselves. Our refusal to do the "work of mourning" destroys much of our capacity to enjoy life, living, and loving. After all, how can we relate to ourselves or others if we don't feel? Moving away from grief results in moving away from ourselves and other people.

The avoidance patterns identified and described in this chapter are as follows:

1. The Postponer,
2. The Displacer,
3. The Replacer,
4. The Minimizer, and
5. The Somaticizer,

1. The Postponer

The postponer is the person who believes that if you delay the expression of your grief, over time it will hopefully go away. Obviously, it does not. The grief builds within and typically comes out in a variety of ways that do not best serve the needs of the mourner.

This person may feel that if the grief doesn't vanish, at least a point in time may come when it will feel safer to experience the pain. Unaware that through expression comes healing, he or she continues to postpone. The grief builds up inside the person pushing toward the point of explosion, thus making him or her feel even less capable of experiencing feelings related to the loss.

Without self-awareness or intervention, a vicious cycle is firmly rooted in place. Often, the more the person senses grief yearning for expression, the more an effort is made to postpone or put off.

Postponing is frequently an automatic unconscious process. A few people will consciously acknowledge this pattern with comments like, "I just don't want to grieve right now. I'll think about it later." However, the majority of people do not know they are postponing the work of their grief. They initiate this pattern of avoidance quietly and quickly, and society often perceives them as "doing very well."

2. The Displacer

The displacer is the person who takes the expression of his or her grief away from the loss itself and displaces the feelings in other directions. For example, while not acknowledging feelings of grief the person may complain of difficulty at work or in relationships with other people. Another example is the person who appears to be chronically agitated and upset at even the most minor of events. While some awareness may be present, displacing usually occurs with total unconsciousness.

Some persons who adopt the displacer orientation become bitter toward life in general. Others displace the bitter unconscious expression of their grief inward and become full of self-hate and experience debilitating depression. So, while at times this person displaces his or her grief in interactions with other people, at other times he or she believes that other people dislike him or her, once again projecting unhappiness from the inside to the outside.

The main intent of the displacer is to shift grief away from its sources and onto a less threatening person, place, or situation. Personal relationships often become stressed and strained for the displacer who is unable to acknowledge the occurrence of this common pattern of grief avoidance.

3. The Replacer

The replacer is the person who takes the emotions that were invested in the relationship that ended in death and reinvests the emotions prematurely in another relationship. Again, little, if any, conscious awareness occurs for this person of how the replacement efforts are really a means of avoiding the work of grief.

Observers from the outside will sometimes assume the replacer must not have loved the person that died all that much if they can so quickly become involved in a new relationship. In actuality, the replacer has often loved very much and out of the need to overcome the pain of confronting feelings related to the loss, moves into an avoidance pattern of replacement.

The replacement pattern does not only occur in relationships with other people. For example, another common replacement appears to be the person who overworks. The compulsive overworker is the person who, with no prior history of doing so, begins to overinvest himself or herself in work to the point where no time is available to think or feel about the loss.

An example of this is a man I recently saw in my practice who, following the death of his wife, found himself working 18 to 20 hours a day. What became apparent was that he was funneling all of the emotions related to his wife's death into and through his work. Once this pattern was acknowledged for the need it was serving him, he could begin to do the work of his mourning in healthy, life-giving ways.

4. The Minimizer

The minimizer is the person who is aware of feelings of grief, but when felt, works to minimize the feelings by diluting them through a variety of rationalizations. This person attempts to prove to self that he or she is not really impacted by the loss that was experienced. Observers of the minimizer may well hear him or her talk about how well he or she is doing and how he or she is back to the normal routine.

On a conscious level his or her minimizations may seem to be working and certainly conform to society's message to quickly "get over" one's grief. However, internally the repressed feelings of grief build within and emotional strain results.

This person often believes that grief is something to be quickly thought through, but not felt through. This is typically an intellectual process in which words become a substitute for the expression of authentic feelings. Any feelings of grief are very threatening to the minimizer who seeks to avoid pain at all costs.

Unfortunately, the more this person works to convince self that the feelings of grief have been "overcome," the more crippled he or she becomes in allowing for emotional expression. The result is the evolution of a destructive, vicious cycle.

5. The Somaticizer

The somaticizer is the person who converts his or her feelings of grief into physical symptoms. This converted physical expression of grief can range from relatively benign minor complaints to the severely malignant chronic pattern of somaticization disorder, i.e., multiple vague somatic complaints with no organic findings.

Unfortunately many people in grief unconsciously adopt the somaticizer role in an effort to get their emotional needs met. By taking on the "sick role" people around them legitimize their very real need to be nurtured and comforted. These persons often fear, that if they were to express their true feelings of grief, people would pull away and leave them feeling abandoned.

Somaticizers may become so completely preoccupied with bodily involvement and sickness that they have little or no energy to relate to others and to do the work of their mourning. Even in the absence of real illness and emotional support from medical caregivers, no amount of reassurance or logic convinces them that they are not "physically sick." The unconscious need to protect oneself requires that this person desperately needs the belief in illness to mask feelings connected to the death.

We should note that the described somaticizer avoidance pattern is different than the person who experiences real physical illness during the mourning process. Some degree of physical disturbance is a common dimension of the normal grief process. As caregivers we would never want to automatically assume that a bereaved person is converting all of his or her emotions into physical symptoms. Numerous investigations have documented a definite physical risk for the griever much greater than that of the nonbereaved population. A general medical examination for bereaved persons is always an excellent standard of care.

CONSEQUENCES OF ADOPTING GRIEF AVOIDANCE PATTERNS

The specific reasons bereaved people adopt grief avoidance patterns are often multiple and complicated. For the purpose of this chapter we will simply note that the major impediments to the healthy expression of grief are usually problems in allowing oneself to feel and to express deep feelings. Some people have struggles with a high need for self-control, others may have an intolerance to feelings of pain and helplessness, while still others may lack a support system that encourages the expression of their feelings.

The result of grief avoidance is a virtual epidemic of complicated and unreconciled grief in our country. This writer's clinical experience suggests that a tremendous amount of anxiety, depression, and physical illness has resulted from many persons' needs to avoid their grief.

Among some of the more common consequences of adopting grief avoidance patterns are the following:

> deterioration in relationships with friends and family;

> symptoms of chronic physical illness whether real or imagined;

> symptoms of chronic depression, sleeping difficulties, and low self-esteem; and

> symptoms of chronic anxiety, agitation, restlessness, and difficulty concentrating.

This list is not intended to be all-inclusive. Different people will experience a wide variety of fall-out consequences from their adoption of avoidance patterns.

ENCOURAGING THE
HEALTHY EXPRESSION OF GRIEF

Healthy mourning is based on an assumption that feelings are best accepted and expressed. Confronting one's grief and the pain inherent in the experience is not always an easy task. However, for reconciliation to occur it is a task that must be done.

One of the reasons for many people's preoccupation with the question, "How long does grief last?" may well be related to society's impatience with grief. Shortly after the funeral the grieving person is expected to "be back to normal." Persons who continue to express grief are often viewed as "weak," "crazy," or "self-pitying." Grief is something to be overcome rather than experienced.

The result of these kinds of messages is encouragement of the repression of the griever's thoughts and feelings and often leads to the adoption of the previously listed grief avoidance response styles. Refusing to allow tears, suffering in silence, and "being strong" are thought to be admirable behaviors. Yet the most healthful approach to grief is to approach it head-on.

The lack of expression of outward mourning has brought about the evolution of "the silent mourner." Even those persons who want to be supportive cannot identify the mourner. The relegating of grief to behind closed doors reinforces the importance of being outreach oriented with one's helping efforts.

All too often our society continues to fail to support the bereaved person, particularly during the lengthy transition period after the funeral. An emphasis on being rational and staying under control influences the mourner to reintegrate into the social network and keep tears, fears, and hurts to himself or herself. We must work to reverse this trend that fails to acknowledge the continuing need for support and understanding of the bereaved.

CHAPTER 21

CHILDREN AND GRIEF

Obviously, funeral directors are often in an excellent position to offer guidance and support to both parents and children during times of death and grief. You have the opportunity to provide compassionate care to bereaved families while embracing the reality that children are frequently the "forgotten mourners."

We now realize that the capacity to grieve does not focus only on one's ability to "understand," but instead upon one's ability to "feel." Any child, regardless of chronological age, that is capable of loving is capable of grieving. While the very young child may not have the ability to comprehend the total meaning of death, primarily because of inability to sense time and space, this inability makes the child's response to acute loss potentially more profound.

Reconciliation to the death of someone loved is typically even more complex for children than for adults. Outward expressions of mourning are not always easily observed in children. Observers expecting to see grief expressed in children in the same way adults mourn unfortunately may assume that children are not influenced by the death. Experience suggests that children usually express grief through behavior as opposed to specific words they might say. Careful observations of behavior will provide cues that illustrate the need for ongoing support, understanding, and guidance.

Among other helping roles, funeral directors can

1. encourage families to include children in the events surrounding death;

2. educate parents regarding typical ways in which children express grief;

3. create an open atmosphere that encourages children to ask questions about death, dying, and grief;

4. develop a caregiving relationship with children that informs them of the funeral director's individual emotional availability to them; and

5. model for children the reality that grief is a privilege that results from the capacity to give and receive love.

Experiences with loss and grief are an integral part of the natural development and growth of the child and the family. The funeral director's willingness and capacity to "be with" the family during times of grief can be difficult, time-consuming, and emotionally draining; however, this time also can be among the most rewarding of caregiving opportunities.

DEVELOPMENTAL CONCEPTS OF DEATH

Like all areas of development, children's capacity to understand death grows and expands as children mature. To this date, in a number of studies tremendous variability has been found regarding the specific age at which a mature understanding of death is achieved (Anthony, 1971; Furman, 1974; Nagy, 1948). This variability appears to be affected by personality factors, sociocultural factors, nature of the death, and probably a multitude of other factors that are unidentified at this time. As a result, caregivers must keep in mind that each child is an individual shaped by experiences of life.

For our current purposes, let us recognize that a number of investigators have attempted to outline various age-level classifications at which specific ideas related to death occur. Outcomes from the investigations lack total agreement on specifics associated with death as determined by the age of the child. However, all investigators do agree that associations move from no understanding toward specifics, which is a developmental concept. Therefore, chronological age is one way of making some attempt to classify what might be expected in terms of understanding death.

In summary, children do appear to proceed from little or no understanding of death to recognition of the concept in realistic form. While most often levels of understanding are listed in chronological order, the individual child may well deviate from the specific age range and particular behavior associated with that age. All of us as careproviders have had the experience of working with some eight-year-olds who are more mature than some sixteen-year-olds with whom we have worked.

While evidence does appear for the age-level understanding of children's concepts of death, one needs to keep in mind that development involves much more than simply growing older. Environmental support, behavior, attitudes, responsiveness of adults, self-concept, intelligence, previous experiences with death, and a number of other factors have an important role in the individual child's understanding of death.

DIMENSIONS OF RESPONSE
TO DEATH

To provide a detailed overview of this area would require that I go beyond the scope of this text. However, for a detailed review of this author's perceptions of children's emotional responses to death, the reader is referred to my text, *Helping Children Cope With Grief* (Wolfelt, 1983). In Figure 21.1 is provided a brief outline of typical responses caregivers are likely to observe in children who are mourning.

CHILDREN AND FUNERALS

Experience suggests that the funeral is a significant occasion in the life of the entire family. Since the funeral is a significant event, children should have the same opportunity to attend as any other member of the family.

SHOCK/DENIAL/DISBELIEF/NUMBNESS

LACK OF FEELINGS

PHYSIOLOGICAL CHANGES

REGRESSION

"BIG MAN" OR "BIG WOMAN" SYNDROME

DISORGANIZATION AND PANIC

EXPLOSIVE EMOTIONS

ACTING-OUT BEHAVIOR

FEAR

GUILT AND SELF-BLAME

RELIEF

LOSS/EMPTINESS/SADNESS

RECONCILIATION

Figure 21.1. Dimensions of childhood grief.

Yes, children should be "allowed" to attend, but never forced. Children can often sense whether adults around them will be able to make the experience a meaningful and comfortable experience and on that basis make a decision to attend or not attend. By encouraging children to be a part of the group sharing of a common loss, we as adults help them acknowledge the reality and finality of death.

An area of discussion that funeral directors can help remind parents to talk about with children is the "why" of going to the funeral. Adults sometimes talk about going to funerals, but fail to talk about why they are going. Encourage parents to explain the purpose of a funeral: as a time to honor the person who has died; as a time to help, comfort, and support each other; and as a time to affirm that life continues.

Children's first visit to a funeral home is often best experienced with only a few people who are especially close. This allows children to react and express feelings freely and to talk about any concerns they might have. Children should be encouraged to ask questions and provided opportunities to do so prior to, during, and after the funeral.

Viewing the body of someone loved also can be a positive experience. Adults would do well to remember that children have no innate fears about the dead body. Seeing the body provides an opportunity to say "good-bye" and helps prevent fears that are often much worse than reality. As with attending the funeral, however, seeing the body should not be forced. While children, particularly young children, may not completely understand the ceremony surrounding death, being involved in the funeral helps establish a sense of comfort and the understanding that life goes on even though someone loved has died.

CHILDREN, RELIGION, AND DEATH

Many families turn to funeral directors for help in this area. While no simple guidelines exist that make this an easy task, the key, as with most experiences in life, appears to be honesty.

Adults can only share with children those concepts they truly believe. You can help parents understand that children need not understand and grasp the total religious philosophy of the adult world. Any religious explanations about death are best described in concrete, practical terms; children have difficulty understanding abstractions. The theological correctness of the information is less important at this time than the fact that the adult is communicating in a loving way. Help parents understand that one need not feel guilty or ashamed if "God" and "Heaven" cannot be explained with exact definitions. Many occurrences in life can be enriched by approaching them with mystery and awe.

CHILDREN, THE FAMILY,
AND MOURNING

Experience suggests that the significant adults in children's lives are the most important factor in allowing and encouraging children to mourn. Children's ability to share their grief outside of themselves depends on the capacity of significant adults expressing their own grief and conveying to children that they too can express a full spectrum of feelings. The sharing of grief between parents and children assists the family in recognizing both the uniqueness and commonality of their experience. This means that the children can learn that Mom and Dad will be sad at times, but that this feeling is normal and not a rejection of the children.

When children experience those times in life when their parents are sad, or hurt, or lonely, or whatever the feeling may be, and also realize that as children they are not responsible for these feelings, the result is that children learn to express freely their own wide range of feelings following loss. Funeral directors are often a vital link in helping families understand the importance of modeling the open expression of feelings. As emphasized as a theme throughout this chapter, pain is healed through the outward expression of mourning. Should significant adults surrounding children fail to share their own loss-related thoughts and feelings, chances are that the children will grieve in isolation while failing to mourn outside of themselves.

OPEN FAMILIES VERSUS
CLOSED FAMILIES

In referring to the "open-system family" I mean those families that permit and encourage the open and honest self-expression of its members. In such a family children are accepted as integral parts of the family and capable of understanding at their own level of development. Children are not seen as little and as a result bad. In such a family, differences in terms of the meaning of the death are viewed as natural and are able to be discussed. In an "open-system family" children can participate in decision making, accept any and all feelings of grief, and say what they think and feel in that grief is viewed as an opportunity for growth.

Conversely in a "closed-system family" children are often encouraged to repress, deny, and hide their grief. The primary rule is that everyone in the family is supposed to think and feel the same way, and as a result, no need exists to talk about thoughts and feelings. In such a family, expression of grief is often impossible, and if it does occur, the expression is viewed as being abnormal or "sick." Children in this kind of family often carry their grief around with them for years and express it in various sorts of emotional and behavioral disturbances.

In summary, caring adults need to communciate to children that feelings of grief are not something to be ashamed of or something to hide. Instead, grief is a natural expression of love for the person who died.

As caring adults, the challenge is clear: children do not choose between grieving and not grieving; adults, on the other hand, do have a choice—to help or not to help children cope with grief. With love, understanding, and knowledge of helping skills, we as adult caregivers can guide children through this vulnerable time and help make the experience a valuable part of children's personal growth and development.

FINAL THOUGHTS

Working in funeral service provides you with a real opportunity to help both adults and children who experience grief and need to mourn. We know that those first few days following a death are critical to the long-term renewal of meaning and purpose in the lives of survivors. Funeral home staffs have a responsibility to not only learn the "mechanics" of sound funeral service practice, but also to learn the "art" of interpersonally helping people who are in grief. Hopefully, this chapter will help you continue to enhance your capacity to "be with" people during one of life's most difficult times.

REFERENCES

Anthony, S. (1971). *The discovery of death in childhood and after.* London: Allan Lan, Penguin.

Furman, E. (1974). *A child's parent dies.* New Haven: Yale University Press.

Nagy, M. (1948). The child's theories concerning death. *Journal of Genetic Psychology, 73:* pp 3-27.

Wolfelt, A. (1983). *Helping children cope with grief.* Muncie, IN: Accelerated Development.

SUMMARY OUTCOMES
OF PART IV

After reading Part IV you should be able to (1) dispel five common myths about grief, (2) outline ten factors that influence the unique response of the mourner, (3) provide an overview of common dimensions of grief, (4) understand five common patterns through which people avoid the "work of mourning," and (5) be able to discuss important concepts regarding children and grief.

PART V

CARING
FOR THE
CAREGIVER

CHAPTER 22

FUNERAL SERVICE AND STRESS: CARING FOR THE CAREGIVER

"Without work all life goes rotten. But when work is soulless, life stifles and dies."

Author Unknown

THE FUNERAL DIRECTOR AND STRESS

A growing awareness is occurring within funeral services of the enormous cost of employees' dissatisfaction both for the individual and the funeral home. For the good of the profession the time has come to focus some efforts on "how to care for the funeral director as caregiver" (Wolfelt, 1989a; 1989b).

Without a doubt, few vocations are more challenging, or more rewarding, than the opportunity to work in funeral service. However, few funeral directors can avoid the special stress that comes with entering into this important field of service.

Assisting people before, during, and after the funeral is a demanding interpersonal process that requires energy, focus, and desire to understand. Working with people in grief forces you to confront your own losses, fears, hopes, and dreams surrounding both life and death.

Whenever you attempt to respond to the needs of people in grief, the chances are slim that you can, or should, avoid the stress of emotional involvement. The key is what you choose to do with the stress and the art of learning how to not only care for others, but yourself.

As you work with people in grief, you open yourself to care about them and their personal journey of mourning. Genuinely caring about the mourner and sharing with him or her some of the most difficult of times in life touches the depths of your own heart and soul.

Specific causes of stress can originate from a variety of sources. Funeral service continues to change rapidly, and change by its nature means stress. Other stresses include intermittent interruption of schedules, the discovery of churned-up feelings related to personal loss of friends and family, time spent away from family and friends, and unrealistic expectations about people always appreciating the value of the service you have to offer.

The result of these influences is potentially what we might term **FUNERAL SERVICE BURNOUT.** Symptoms of this burnout syndrome often include the following:

1. exhaustion and loss of energy,

2. irritability and impatience,

3. cynicism and detachment,

4. physical complaints and depression,

5. disorientation and confusion,

6. omnipotence and feeling indispensable, and

7. minimization and denial of feelings.

The purpose of this chapter is to outline these stress-related signs and symptoms. In addition we will address how funeral directors can strive to take care of themselves and avoid becoming "wounded healers."

EXHAUSTION AND LOSS OF ENERGY

Feelings of exhaustion and loss of energy are usually among the first signals of funeral director stress. Low energy and fatigue for the funeral director is often difficult to acknowledge because this is the opposite of the high energy level required to meet demands that are both self-imposed and experienced from the outside.

Our bodies are powerful instruments and frequently much wiser than our minds. Exhaustion and lack of physical and psychic energy are often unconscious "self cries for help." Now, if we could only slow down and listen to the temple within.

IRRITABILITY AND IMPATIENCE

As stress builds from within, irritability and impatience become inherent components of the experience of "funeral service burnout." As an effective helper, you have typically experienced a sense of accomplishment and reward for your efforts. As stress increases, the ability to feel reward diminishes while your irritability and impatience become heightened.

Disagreements and tendencies to blame others for any interpersonal difficulties may occur as stress takes its toll on your sense of emotional and physical well-being. A real sign to watch for is that you have more care to give the families you serve than you have compassion and sensitivity to the needs of your own family.

CYNICISM AND DETACHMENT

As funeral directors experiencing emotional burn-out, you may begin to respond to stress in a manner that saves something of yourself. You may begin to question the value of funeral service, of your family life, of friendships, even of life itself. You may work to create distance between yourself and the families you are serving.

You may work to convince yourself, "There is no point in getting involved" as you rationalize your need to distance yourself from the stress of interpersonal encounter. Detachment serves to help distance yourself from feelings of pain, helplessness, and hurt.

PHYSICAL COMPLAINTS
AND DEPRESSION

Physical complaints, real or imagined, are often experienced in funeral directors suffering from burnout. Sometimes, physical complaints are easier to talk about than emotional concerns. The process of consciously or unconsciously converting emotional conflicts may result in a variety of somatic symptoms like headaches, stomachaches, backaches, and long-lasting colds. These symptoms are direct cues related to the potential of stress overload.

Generalized feelings of depression also are common to the phenomenon of "funeral service burnout." Loss of appetite, difficulty sleeping, sudden changes in mood, and lethargy suggest that depression has become a part of the overall stress syndrome. Depression is a constellation of symptoms that tell you something is wrong to which you need to pay attention and work to understand.

DISORIENTATION AND CONFUSION

Feelings of disorientation and confusion are often experienced as a component of this syndrome. Your mind may shift from one topic to another, and focusing on current tasks often becomes difficult. You may experience "polyphasic behavior," whereby you feel busy, yet do not accomplish much at all. Since difficulty focusing results in a lack of personal sense of competence, confusion only results in more heightened feelings of disorientation.

Thus, a cycle of confusion resulting in more disorientation evolves and becomes difficult to break. The ability to think clearly suffers, and concentration and memory are impaired. In addition, the ability to make decisions and sound judgements becomes limited. Obviously your system is overloaded and in need of a break from the continuing cycle of stress.

OMNIPOTENCE AND
FEELING INDISPENSABLE

Another common symptom of what this author has termed "funeral service burnout" is a sense of omnipotence and feeling indispensable. Statements like, "No one else can make arrangements like I can," or, "I have got to be the one to help all those people in grief" are not simply the expressions of a normal ego.

Other funeral directors can be helpful to families and may do it very well. This author acknowledges that in a small firm you may be the only one available.

However, if you as a funeral director begin to feel indispensable, you typically block your own, as well as others', growth. Thinking that no one else can provide adequate help to families but oneself is, among other things, often an indication of stress overload.

MINIMIZATION AND
DENIAL OF FEELINGS

Some funeral directors when stressed to their limits continue to minimize, if not deny, feelings of burnout. The person who minimizes is aware of feeling stressed, but when felt, works to minimize the feelings by diluting them through a variety of rationalizations. From a self perspective, minimizing stress seems to work, particularly because it is commensurate with the self-imposed helping principle of "being all things to all people." However, internally repressed feelings of stress build within and emotional strain results.

Perhaps the most dangerous characteristic of the "funeral service burnout syndrome" is the total denial of feelings of stress. As denial takes over, the funeral director's symptoms of stress become enemies to be fought instead of friends to be understood. Regardless of how loud the mind and body cry out for relief, no one is listening.

The specific reasons funeral directors adopt denial of feelings of stress are often multiple and complex. For the purposes of this article we will note that when you care deeply for people in grief, you open yourself to your own vulnerabilities related to loss issues. Perhaps another person's grief stimulates memories of some old griefs of your own. Perhaps those you wish to help through the experience of the funeral frustrate your efforts to be supportive.

Whatever the reason, the natural way to prevent yourself from being hurt or disappointed is to deny feelings in general. This denial of feelings is often accompanied by an internal sense of a lack of purpose in what you are doing. After all, the willingness and ability to feel are ultimately what gives meaning to life.

This outline of potential symptoms is not intended to be all-inclusive or mutually exclusive. The majority of overstressed funeral directors will experience a combination of symptoms. The specific combination of symptoms will vary dependent on such influences as basic personality and outside influences.

Of all the stresses inherent in funeral directors, emotional involvements appear central to the potential of suffering from burnout. Perhaps we should ask ourselves what we lose when we decide to minimize or ignore the significant level of emotional involvement that occurs when working in funeral service.

We probably will discover that in the process of minimizing or ignoring we are, in fact, depleting our potential to help of this most important component: the all powerful reality that **caring about people in grief** while at the same time **caring for oneself** is vital to helping people during these difficult times. While the admirable goal of helping others may seem to justify emotional sacrifices, ultimately we are not helping others effectively when we ignore what we are experiencing within ourselves.

If you acknowledge that effective interpersonal helping is always tied to the relationship you establish with families served, then you also must focus on yourself as you are involved with the people you are assisting. This relates to the demanding dual focus that is essential to being an effective funeral director to the bereaved. As the saying goes, "If you want to help others, the place to start is with yourself."

Experience suggests that practice is needed to work toward an understanding of what is taking place inside yourself while trying to grasp what is taking place inside others. After all, these thoughts and feelings occur simultaneously and are significantly interrelated.

Obviously, you cannot draw close to others without beginning to affect and be affected by them. This is the nature of helping relationships with bereaved families. We cannot help others from a protective position. Helping occurs openly where you are defenseless, if you allow yourself to be. Again, this double focus on the mourner and on oneself is essential to the art of being an effective funeral director.

As caregivers to the living and the dead, an important recognition is that on occasion you too may need a supportive relationship where you can be listened to and accepted—to recharge your emotional battery. Few people who have ever tried to respond to the needs of others in a helping relationship have escaped the stress that comes from emotional involvement.

Involving yourself with others, particularly at a time of death and grief, requires taking care of oneself as well as others. Emotional overload, intermittent interruption of schedules, circumstances surrounding deaths, and caring about people will ultimately result in times of "funeral service burnout." When this occurs, you should feel no sense of inadequacy or stigma if you also need the support and understanding of a caring relationship. As a matter of fact, you should be proud of yourself if you care enough about "caring for the funeral director as a caregiver" that you seek out just such a relationship!

AM I EXPERIENCING
FUNERAL SERVICE BURNOUT?

Very little documented research is available that compares levels of stress and potential burnout across different professions. However, the general concensus is that funeral directors experience burnout on a routine basis.

A funeral director recently inquired, "How is burnout different from stress?" We might overhear someone comment, "I'm really feeling burned-out today." All of us may have occasional days when our motivation and energy levels vary. While this fluctuation in energy states is normal, burnout is an end stage that typically develops over time. Once a person is "burned-out," dramatic changes become vital to reversing the process.

Psychologist Christina Maslach (1982), a leading authority on burnout, has outlined three major qualities of burnout.

Emotional Exhaustion—feeling drained, not having anything to give even before the day begins.

Depersonalization—feeling disconnected from other people, feeling resentful and seeing them negatively.

Reduced Sense of Personal Accomplishment—feeling ineffective, that the results achieved are not meaningful.

Step back for a moment and complete what we will term the "Brief Funeral Service Burnout Survey" (BFSBS) provided in Figure 22.1. As you review your life over the past 12 months answer the survey questions.

To monitor your potential for burnout, ask yourself to how many of these questions you answered "yes." In general, if you answered "yes" to two to four of these questions, you are standing too close to the fire. If you answered "yes" to five to seven of these questions, call the fire department because you're burned-out. If you answered "yes" to eight to ten of these questions, your feet are in the flame.

BRIEF FUNERAL SERVICE BURNOUT SURVEY
(BFSBS)
Alan D. Wolfelt, Ph.D.

Yes   **No**

_____ _____ 1. Do you generally feel more fatigued and lacking in energy?

_____ _____ 2. Are you getting more irritable, impatient, and angry with people around you (home and/or work)?

_____ _____ 3. Do you feel more cynical and detached from the people with whom you work?

_____ _____ 4. Are you experiencing more than your share of physical complaints like headaches, stomachaches, backaches, and long-lasting colds?

_____ _____ 5. Do you generally feel more depressed or notice sudden fluctuations in your moods?

_____ _____ 6. Do you feel busy, yet have a sense that you don't accomplish much at all?

_____ _____ 7. Are you suffering from difficulties in the areas of concentration or memory?

_____ _____ 8. Do you think that you have to be the one to help every family that comes through the door?

_____ _____ 9. Do you feel less of a sense of satisfaction about your helping efforts?

_____ _____ 10. Do you feel that you just don't have anything more to give to people?

Figure 22.1. Brief Funeral Service Burnout Survey (BFSBS).

GUIDELINES FOR CARING FOR
THE FUNERAL DIRECTOR

The following practical guidelines are not intended to be all-inclusive. Pick and choose those tips that you believe will be of help to you in your efforts to stay physically and emotionally healthy.

Remember, our attitudes in general about stress and burnout sometimes make it difficult to make changes. However, one important point to remember is that with support and encouragement from others, most of us can learn to make positive changes in our attitudes and behaviors.

You might find that having a discussion among coworkers about this topic of funeral service burnout is helpful. Identify your own signs and symptoms of burnout. Discuss individual and group approaches to self-care that will help you enjoy both work and play!

The following guidelines can be meaningful in assisting you to prevent burnout. Reread these guidelines frequently to help yourself reassess development and performance:

1. Recognize that you are working in an area of care where the risk of burnout is high. While working in funeral service has its rewards, it also has its dangers. Keeping yourself aware that you are "at risk" for burnout will help keep you from denying the existence of stress-related signs and symptoms.

2. Create periods of rest and renewal. The quickest way to burnout is spreading yourself too thin—trying to help too many people or taking on too many tasks. Learn to respect both your mind and body's needs for periods of rest after helping other people.

3. Be compassionate with yourself about not being perfect. After all, none of us are! As people who like to help others, we may think our helping efforts should always be successful. Some people will reject your help while others will be invested in minimizing the significance of your

help. This is particularly true in people who do not perceive value in having a funeral service. Also remind yourself that mistakes are an integral part of learning and growth, but are not reflections of your self-worth.

4. Practice setting limits and alleviate stresses you can do something about. Work to achieve a clear sense of expectations and set realistic deadlines. Enjoy what you do accomplish in helping others, and do not berate yourself for what is beyond you.

5. Learn effective time-management skills. Set practical goals for how you spend your time. Don't allow time to become an enemy. When working on projects remember Pareto's principle: 20 percent of what you do nets 80 percent of your results.

6. Work to cultivate a personal support system. A close personal friend can be a real lifesaver when it comes to managing stress and preventing burnout. If you have already reached the crisis state of burnout, realize that you may well need the help of others in making life-style changes. Many funeral directors have trouble asking for help. If this is the case for you, practice giving yourself permission to seek outside support. Remember, recent research has demonstrated that human companionship and connectedness helps you live longer.

7. Express the personal you in both your work and play. Don't be afraid to demonstrate your unique talents and abilities. Make time each day to remind yourself of what is important to you. Act on what you believe is important. If you only had three months to live, what would you do? Use this question to help determine what is really important in the big picture of life and living.

8. Work to understand your motivation to work in funeral service. Does your need to help others with grief relate in any way to your own unreconciled losses? If so, be certain not to use your helping relationships to work on your own grief. Find trusted resources to help you work with any old and new losses.

9. Develop healthy eating, sleeping, and exercise patterns. We are often aware of the importance of these areas for those we help; however, as caregivers we sometimes neglect them ourselves. A well-balanced diet, adequate sleep, and regular exercise allows for our own physical, mental, and emotional well-being.

10. Strive to identify the unique ways in which your body informs you that you are stressed. Do you get tightness in the shoulders, backaches, headaches? Becoming conscious of how your body communicates stress signals to you allows for awareness of stressful situations before they overwhelm you. A constant state of physical tension often results in deterioration, which results in physical breakdown.

FINAL THOUGHTS

Again, be aware that the above practical guidelines are not intended to be all-inclusive. This author suggests that you and your colleagues develop your own list of how to prevent and work with "funeral service burnout."

Each one of us has our own unique style of relating to the stresses of living. Sometimes we manage those stresses well, while at other times we need people who care about us to help us to acknowledge the potential of burnout. Hopefully, this chapter will assist you in assessing your own stress level and, if appropriate, help you begin to make some changes.

No doubt exists in this author's mind and heart that to work in funeral service is a true privilege. Perhaps we can be proud that we want to help make a difference in people's lives, while at the same time remembering the importance of taking care of ourselves as caregivers.

Caring about our life's work, even enjoying it, will probably seem strange if we only see it as a way to make a living. However, if we can see our work as a way to enrich each moment of our living, we may well discover a deep caring within our souls that teaches us to learn and grow each and every day.

```
┌─────────────────────────────────────────────────────┐
│                     ACTIVITY 22.1                    │
│                 PERSONAL SIGNS OF STRESS             │
│                 AND SELF-CARE STRATEGIES             │
│                                                       │
│ Directions                                            │
│                                                       │
│     Form small groups of three to five people. Each  │
│ person can express three personal symptoms that they │
│ know they experience when stressed. Each person will │
│ then list three self-care strategies that he or she  │
│ uses to manage stress.                                │
│                                                       │
│ Expectations                                          │
│                                                       │
│     By sharing personal symptoms and management      │
│ strategies group members will gain new insights into │
│ stress producers and means to prevent burnout.       │
│                                                       │
└─────────────────────────────────────────────────────┘
```

SUMMARY OUTCOMES
OF CHAPTER

After reading and participating in the activities related to this chapter you should be able to (1) outline several specific causes of stress in funeral service, (2) identify seven stress-related signs and symptoms, (3) acknowledge if you are personally experiencing "funeral service burnout," and (4) discuss practical self-care guidelines for surviving stress and enjoying life!

REFERENCES

Maslach, C. (1982). Understanding burn-out: Definitional issues in analyzing a complex phenomenon, in W.S. Paine (Ed.), *Job stress and burn-out.* Beverly Hills, CA: Sage Publications.

Wolfelt, A.D. (1989a). Funeral service burn-out: Signs and symptoms, *The Director,* November.

Wolfelt, A. (1989b). Survival techniques, *The Director,* December.

Additional Resource

To receive a descriptive brochure of Dr. Wolfelt's annual "Caring for the Caregiver" Seminar that is held in May of each year in the Virgin Islands, write the Center for Loss and Life Transition, 3735 Broken Bow Road, Fort Collins, Colorado 80526 (Telephone 303/226-6050).

CHAPTER **23**

A FINAL WORD

"We can be cured of depression in only fourteen days if every day we will try to think how we can be helpful to others."

Alfred Adler

Hopefully, the material outlined in this book will allow you to be even more prepared for your helping responsibilities with people—before, during, and after the funeral. You have the opportunity to "be with" people during times of great emotional distress, including the "first call," the arrangement conference, the first viewing, the funeral service and committal, as well as the post-funeral period. What an opportunity to help other human beings!

Yes, other trained professionals are available to offer support and assistance; however, none are in a better position to provide help during the entire experience of death than you— the funeral director. You are not usurping the role of other helping professionals, but rather you have purposeful, immediate, and ongoing access to the grieving family. If you have developed a helping-healing relationship during the funeral experience, your presence and help will be welcomed by the grieving family long after the death has occurred.

Building helping skills as you have done through this training experience augments your overall abilities as a funeral director and assists you in becoming an indispensable member of the community of caregiving professionals. When people need help beyond your skills, you are in the natural position to provide appropriate referral to other community resources.

Using your new skills to reach out and assist others will build your confidence as a helper. Just as those funeral directors who have poor communication skills often become natural targets for the grieving person's frustration and helplessness, those with effective communication skills will be rewarded by the people served.

While helping has its rewards, it also has its hazards. The helping process requires energy and focus. It is also a demanding interpersonal experience. Fortunately, you can help yourself cope with the stress that comes from being a helper. The result is that helping becomes an exciting and rewarding endeavor.

As a helping funeral director, recognize that on occasions you too need a supportive relationship where you can be listened to and accepted—to recharge your emotional battery. Few people who have ever tried to respond to the needs of others in a helping relationship have escaped the stress that comes from emotional involvement. Involving yourself with others, particularly at a time of death and grief, requires taking care of oneself as well as others.

As noted in Chapter 22, emotional overload, circumstances surrounding deaths, and caring about people will ultimately touch the depths of your own heart. When this occurs, you should feel no sense of inadequacy or stigma if you, too, need the support and understanding of a caring relationship.

Also critically important is to realize that you don't have to help everyone, with everything, all of the time. Should you find yourself doing this, chances are before long you will have little to give in any of your helping relationships. In some situations your effectiveness as a helper will naturally be limited. Also recognize that on some occasions people will not allow you to be helpful. Acknowledge that these circumstances exist and do not expect more of yourself than (1) what you have to give and (2) what people will allow you to give.

You also will find that working toward an understanding of what is taking place inside yourself is very important, while trying to grasp what is taking place inside others. After all, these thoughts and feelings occur simultaneously; they are often significantly interrelated. Obviously you cannot draw close to others without beginning to affect and be affected by them. This is the nature of helping relationships. You cannot help others from a protective position. Helping occurs openly where you are defenseless—if you allow yourself to be. This double focus on others as well as yourself is essential to the task of being an effective helper.

What might happen if you were to minimize the stresses involved in helping relationships? You may, in fact, drain your helping potential of the most significant ingredient: the capacity to emotionally involve yourself in an empathetic relationship and enjoy it. Few things are worse than working with people and not enjoying it.

Finally, remember people who seek your help as a funeral director are giving you the highest compliment of which they are capable—they are trusting you to assist them at a difficult time in their lives. Being able to help them is a true privilege, and the potential rewards are many. Preparing yourself to help as best you can speaks of your commitment to this privilege.

Yes, as a funeral director, you are a caretaker of the living, as well as the dead. The development of self-confidence in the area of interpersonal skills will prove to be a tremendous asset, for yourself and the profession as well.

ACTIVITY 23.1
MOVING TOWARD CLOSURE:
GIFT GIVING

Directions

The group sits in a circle: Each participant receives a stack of 3 X 5 cards. The trainer makes the following statement, "We have all come together to work on improving our interpersonal skills. I would like to have us all leave by leaving behind a small gift for each other."

Activity 23.1 (Continued)

The trainer then invites each person to write a message to each participant on an individual 3 X 5 card. The message should be a gift that is intended to make that person feel positive about himself or herself. The message could be the observation of a positive interpersonal quality or skill the person has.

When all participants have finished, they write their first names on an extra card and take off their shoes, placing the name card in one shoe so that it can be easily read. Then they deliver their 3 X 5 cards to the others, placing their cards in the empty shoes.

Expectations

Each group member will collect his or her own 3 X 5 cards (gifts), put on their shoes, and leave.

TRAINING OPPORTUNITIES

Training opportunities related to the content of this book are available through the Center For Loss and Life Transition. Custom programs are often designed to meet the unique needs of particular funeral homes, funeral home organizations, and state associations. The training can be held in your funeral home, or staff members can travel to the Center For Loss and Life Transition.

To inquire about the Center's training opportunities write or telephone:

Center for Loss and Life Transition
3735 Broken Bow Road
Fort Collins, Colorado   80526
Telephone 303-226-6050

INDEX

INDEX

A

Accomplishment
    reduced sense of 196
Adler, A. 203
American Institute for Research
    10, 11
Anthony, S. 180, 186
Anxiety 155-6
Approaches to helping 31
Aristotle 123
Attending, skill 49-63
    See skill, attending
Authentic 42-3
Author
    challenge from 7-8
Avoidance patterns 172-6

B

Barriers
    communication 117-22
    implementation 115-31
    overcoming 115-31
Beginton, H. 23
Behavior
    attending skill 51-7
    bizarre 153
    communication 45
    ethical 32
    questioning 91-2
Bereaved person
    characteristics 145
Bombarding
    questions, with 118
Book
    activities 3
    practical skills 3
    principles 3
    reason for 3-8
    workshop setting 7
Bowlby, H. 157, 170
Bowlby, J. 151, 155, 170
Brammer, L. 31, 32
Brief Funeral Service Burnout Survey
    (BFSBS), *Figure* 197

Burnout
    experiencing 196
    funeral service 190, 96
    prevent 198-200
    survey 196, *Figure* 197
    symptoms 190

C

Care
    for self 189-202
    for funeral director 189-202
Caregiver
    caring for 187-206
Caring 27-8
    description 27
    dimension of 28
Carkhuff, R. 30, 32
Challenge
    from the author 7-8
Changes
    physiological 156-7
Characteristics
    bereaved person 145
    helper 30-2
    helping 24-9
    levels of helping, *Figure* 25
    of helping 23-32
    person who died 145-6
    rating, *Figure* 25
Children
    death 183
    family 184
    first visit to a funeral home 183
    funerals 181-3
    grief 179-86
    mourning 184
    religion 183
    viewing the body 183
Clarifying skill 71-6
    See skill, clarifying
Combs, A. 31, 32
Commitment 50
Communication
    barriers 117-22
    behaviors 45
    levels 43-4

Alan D. Wolfelt, Ph.D.

ABOUT THE AUTHOR

Dr. Alan D. Wolfelt is a noted author, educator, and practicing clinical thanatologist. He is the founder and director of the Center for Loss and Life Transition in Fort Collins, Colorado. He is known throughout the United States and Canada as a long-time friend of funeral service. His background of having lived and worked in a funeral home for seven years makes him uniquely qualified to have written this text.

Many funeral homes, funeral home organizations, and state associations use Dr. Wolfelt as an educational consultant. He is known internationally for his work in the areas of adult and childhood grief. His interest in "helping funeral directors be the best that they can be" stimulated his interest in providing a practical text on interpersonal skills training for funeral home staffs.

A respected author, Alan serves as the editor of the "Children and Grief" department of *Bereavement Magazine* and writes "Thanatologist's Corner" for the journal *Thanatos*. Among his books are *Helping Children Cope with Grief* and *Death and Grief: A Guide for Clergy*. Recent publications include a series of helpful brochures that funeral homes make available to the general public. In addition, he just completed a new series of cassette tapes on death and grief for bereavement caregivers.